OPPOSING VIEWPOINTS® SERIES

Hate Groups and Hate Speech

Other Books of Related Interest

Opposing Viewpoints Series

Antisemitism and Islamophobia
Diversity, Equity, and Inclusion
Identity Politics
Toxic Masculinity
Transnational Repression and Extrajudicial Killings

At Issue Series

Domestic Terrorism
Gender Politics
The Media's Influence on Society
Open Borders
Policing in America

Current Controversies Series

Antifa and the Radical Left
Hate Groups
Historical Revisionism
Holocaust Deniers and Conspiracy Theorists
Nativism, Nationalism, and Patriotism

> "Congress shall make no law … abridging the freedom of speech, or of the press."
>
> ***First Amendment to the U.S. Constitution***

The basic foundation of our democracy is the First Amendment guarantee of freedom of expression. The Opposing Viewpoints series is dedicated to the concept of this basic freedom and the idea that it is more important to practice it than to enshrine it.

Opposing Viewpoints® Series

Hate Groups and Hate Speech

Lisa Idzikowski, Book Editor

Greenhaven Publishing

Published in 2025 by Greenhaven Publishing, LLC
2544 Clinton Street,
Buffalo NY 14224

First Edition

Articles in Greenhaven Publishing anthologies are often edited for length to meet page requirements. In addition, original titles of these works are changed to clearly present the main thesis and to explicitly indicate the author's opinion. Every effort is made to ensure that Greenhaven Publishing accurately reflects the original intent of the authors. Every effort has been made to trace the owners of the copyrighted material.

Cover image: Spondylolithesis/iStockphoto.com

Library of Congress CataloginginPublication Data

Names: Idzikowski, Lisa, editor.
Title: Hate groups and hate speech / edited by Lisa Idzikowski.
Description: First edition. | New York : Greenhaven Publishing, 2025. | Series: Opposing viewpoints | Includes index.
Identifiers: ISBN 9781534510074 (pbk.) | ISBN 9781534510081 (library bound)
Subjects: LCSH: Hate groups. | Hate speech. | Hate crimes.
Classification: LCC HV6773.5 H384 2025 | DDC 305.5680973--dc23

Manufactured in the United States of America

Website: http://greenhavenpublishing.com

Contents

The Importance of Opposing Viewpoints

Perhaps every generation experiences a period in time in which the populace seems especially polarized, starkly divided on the important issues of the day and gravitating toward the far ends of the political spectrum and away from a consensus-facilitating middle ground. The world that today's students are growing up in and that they will soon enter into as active and engaged citizens is deeply fragmented in just this way. Issues relating to terrorism, immigration, women's rights, minority rights, race relations, health care, taxation, wealth and poverty, the environment, policing, military intervention, the proper role of government—in some ways, perennial issues that are freshly and uniquely urgent and vital with each new generation—are currently roiling the world.

If we are to foster a knowledgeable, responsible, active, and engaged citizenry among today's youth, we must provide them with the intellectual, interpretive, and critical-thinking tools and experience necessary to make sense of the world around them and of the all-important debates and arguments that inform it. After all, the outcome of these debates will in large measure determine the future course, prospects, and outcomes of the world and its peoples, particularly its youth. If they are to become successful members of society and productive and informed citizens, students need to learn how to evaluate the strengths and weaknesses of someone else's arguments, how to sift fact from opinion and fallacy, and how to test the relative merits and validity of their own opinions against the known facts and the best possible available information. The landmark series Opposing Viewpoints has been providing students with just such critical-thinking skills and exposure to the debates surrounding society's most urgent contemporary issues for many years, and it continues to serve this essential role with undiminished commitment, care, and rigor.

The key to the series's success in achieving its goal of sharpening students' critical-thinking and analytic skills resides in its title—

Opposing Viewpoints. In every intriguing, compelling, and engaging volume of this series, readers are presented with the widest possible spectrum of distinct viewpoints, expert opinions, and informed argumentation and commentary, supplied by some of today's leading academics, thinkers, analysts, politicians, policy makers, economists, activists, change agents, and advocates. Every opinion and argument anthologized here is presented objectively and accorded respect. There is no editorializing in any introductory text or in the arrangement and order of the pieces. No piece is included as a "straw man," an easy ideological target for cheap point-scoring. As wide and inclusive a range of viewpoints as possible is offered, with no privileging of one particular political ideology or cultural perspective over another. It is left to each individual reader to evaluate the relative merits of each argument—as he or she sees it, and with the use of ever-growing critical-thinking skills—and grapple with his or her own assumptions, beliefs, and perspectives to determine how convincing or successful any given argument is and how the reader's own stance on the issue may be modified or altered in response to it.

This process is facilitated and supported by volume, chapter, and selection introductions that provide readers with the essential context they need to begin engaging with the spotlighted issues, with the debates surrounding them, and with their own perhaps shifting or nascent opinions on them. In addition, guided reading and discussion questions encourage readers to determine the authors' point of view and purpose, interrogate and analyze the various arguments and their rhetoric and structure, evaluate the arguments' strengths and weaknesses, test their claims against available facts and evidence, judge the validity of the reasoning, and bring into clearer, sharper focus the reader's own beliefs and conclusions and how they may differ from or align with those in the collection or those of their classmates.

Research has shown that reading comprehension skills improve dramatically when students are provided with compelling, intriguing, and relevant "discussable" texts. The subject matter of these collections could not be more compelling, intriguing, or urgently relevant to today's students and the world they are poised to inherit. The anthologized articles and the reading and discussion questions that are included with them also provide the basis for stimulating, lively, and passionate classroom debates. Students who are compelled to anticipate objections to their own argument and identify the flaws in those of an opponent read more carefully, think more critically, and steep themselves in relevant context, facts, and information more thoroughly. In short, using discussable text of the kind provided by every single volume in the Opposing Viewpoints series encourages close reading, facilitates reading comprehension, fosters research, strengthens critical thinking, and greatly enlivens and energizes classroom discussion and participation. The entire learning process is deepened, extended, and strengthened.

For all of these reasons, Opposing Viewpoints continues to be exactly the right resource at exactly the right time—when we most need to provide readers with the critical-thinking tools and skills that will not only serve them well in school but also in their careers and their daily lives as decision-making family members, community members, and citizens. This series encourages respectful engagement with and analysis of opposing viewpoints and fosters a resulting increase in the strength and rigor of one's own opinions and stances. As such, it helps make readers "future ready," and that readiness will pay rich dividends for the readers themselves, for the citizenry, for our society, and for the world at large.

Introduction

> *"In recent years, the world has witnessed several mass atrocities. In many of these cases, hate speech was identified as a "precursor to atrocity crimes, including genocide." While the use of social media and digital platforms to spread hatred is relatively recent, the weaponization of public discourse for political gain is unfortunately not new. As history continues to show, hate speech coupled with disinformation can lead to stigmatization, discrimination and large-scale violence."*
>
> — *United Nations*

Hate speech and hate groups, and the controversy surrounding them, are nothing new. Around the world, hate in various forms has been evident since antiquity. Greeks, Romans, and early Christians held Jews in contempt, which has led some people to label antisemitism "history's oldest hatred." The Crusades were fought against Muslims. Armenians became a target around World War I, while Hitler and his Nazis targeted Jews during the Holocaust. America's Civil War was fought because of slavery, and in the 1921 Tulsa Race Massacre, violent mobs attacked, destroyed, and killed black residents, businesses, schools, and homes.

According to the United Nations, hate speech refers to offensive language which targets an individual or a group based on certain characteristics such as gender, religion, or race. A hate group, as explained by the Anti-Defamation League, is any organization whose goals are based on shared hatred toward people of different races, religions, sexual identities, genders, or ethnicities.

Although hate speech and hate groups may not be a solely modern phenomenon, modern culture, politics, and media have an outsized impact on them. The Southern Poverty Law Center documented over 1,300 hate and antigovernment extremist groups in the United States in 2024. According to the FBI's September 2024 report, hate-based crimes had increased from 2023, with those rooted in race, ancestry, or ethnicity being the most commonly occurring.

Notably, politics and media play a role in hate speech and hate groups. Politicians around the world and throughout history have used dislike of certain groups to rally their supporters. Adolf Hitler referred to Jewish people as parasites, blood suckers, and bacteria. With his notions of hatred and propaganda, he rallied the German people to support his evil actions. In 1971, then-governor Ronald Reagan referred to African delegates to the United Nations as "monkeys." Some people have said that President Donald Trump echoed Hitler when he referred to his political enemies as "vermin" at a rally in November of 2023. One thing is certain—experts agree that when politicians weave hate speech into their political rhetoric, violence often follows.

Social media is another factor that affects the type and prevalence of hate speech. Many people use this modern technology for good reasons, such as connecting with friends and famly members, but others use it to amplify hate speech and recruit individuals to join hate groups. Some argue that social media sites and their executives should be responsible for enforcing regulations against hate speech and other forms of hate. However, it is well known that social media rakes in more money when its users are engaged for longer periods, and unfortunately, extreme speech often pulls in extended view times for media platforms.

With so many different factors affecting the problem, many people wonder whether anything can be done to diminish hate speech. Experts agree that one of the best things that can be done is to teach tolerance. This can happen in schools, universities, church settings, and at home. UNICEF advises parents to encourage their children to have a natural curiosity of others, which may counter hate based on false information about other people.

The very timely debate surrounding the issue of hate speech and hate groups is explored in *Opposing Viewpoints: Hate Speech and Hate Groups*, shedding light on this divisive and ongoing contemporary issue.

OPPOSING VIEWPOINTS® SERIES

Chapter 1

Hate Groups in the Past and Present

Chapter Preface

Hatred and hate groups are alive and expanding in the United States. According to the Southern Poverty Law Center, there are more than 1,000 active hate and extremist groups operating across the United States. Although these numbers reflect hate groups acting now, it by no means implies that these groups are only a modern phenomenon.

This chapter addresses the historic roots of hate and the ways hatred of various groups has changed—or not—over time. Several viewpoint articles outline and analyze the increase of hate and hate groups in the United States.

Who is the target of these hate groups? Who engages in this behavior, or joins groups involved in this behavior? Several viewpoint authors examine and explain the types of people that seem to gravitate toward these aberrant activities. Other viewpoint authors examine groups in Europe that have historically been targets of hate, and how this hatred has continued and evolved into modern times. Another viewpoint author investigates how certain immigrant communities living in the United States are the objects of hatemongering.

Viewpoint 1

> *"...the internet and social media have made the problem of white supremacist hate far worse and more visible; it's both more accessible and, ultimately, more violent..."*

White Nationalism Is Increasing

Sophie Bjork-James

In the following viewpoint, Sophie Bjork-James maintains that white nationalism is on the rise. Bjork-James presents statistics to back up her claims of rising membership in violent groups. She also outlines how white supremacy groups pivoted from the 1990s to gain increased membership via social media and the internet. Sophie Bjork-James is an assistant professor of anthropology at Vanderbilt University and has over ten years' experience researching the white supremacist movement. Her work has been featured in many media outlets. including NBC, NPR, BBC, Reuters, The New York Times, *and others.*

As you read, consider the following questions:

1. What has made white supremacist hate worse, according to the author?
2. As stated by the viewpoint, what conspiracy theory do many Republicans believe in?

"Fueled by virtually unrestricted social media access, white nationalism is on the rise and attracting violent young white men" by Sophie Bjork-James, *The Conversation,* August 2, 2022.

3. According to Bjork-James, why are young men joining groups associated with white nationalism?

White nationalists keep showing up in the hearings of the U.S. House committee investigating the Jan. 6, 2021, insurrection.

Evidence is mounting that white nationalist groups who want to establish an all-white state played a significant role in the violent attack on the U.S. Capitol that left five dead and dozens wounded.

Thus far, the hearings "have documented how the Proud Boys helped lead the insurrectionist mob into the U.S. Capitol building in Washington, D.C," journalist James Risen wrote in the *Intercept.*

Based on July 12, 2022, testimony from a former Oath Keepers member, the white nationalist group coordinated with the Three Percenters, another group of white nationalists, and the Proud Boys in mobilizing their extremists groups to rally in Washington, D.C., on Jan. 6, as asked by President Trump in his Dec. 16, 2020, tweet.

As a cultural anthropologist who has studied these movements for over a decade, I know that membership in these organizations is not limited to the attempted violent overthrow of the government and poses an ongoing threat, as seen in massacres carried out by young men radicalized by this movement.

In 2020, for instance, the Department of Homeland Security described domestic violent extremists as "presenting the most persistent and lethal threat" to the people of the United States and the nation's government.

In March 2021, FBI Director Christopher Wray testified to Congress that the number of arrests of white supremacists and other racially motivated extremists has almost tripled since he took office in 2017.

"Jan. 6 was not an isolated event," Wray testified before the Senate Judiciary Committee. "The problem of domestic terrorism has been metastasizing across the country for a long time now, and it's not going away anytime soon."

The Southern Poverty Law Center, a nonprofit civil rights group, tracked 733 active hate groups across the United States in 2021.

Based on my research, the internet and social media have made the problem of white supremacist hate far worse and more visible; it's both more accessible and, ultimately, more violent, as seen on Jan. 6 at the U.S. Capitol and the shooting deaths of ten Black people at a Buffalo grocery story, among other examples.

An expansive, online network

In the 1990s, former KKK leaders including David Duke rebranded white supremacy for the digital age.

They switched KKK robes for business suits and connected neo-Nazi antisemitic conspiracies with broader anti-Black, anti-immigrant and anti-Islamic racism.

From the 1990s to the late 2000s, this movement largely built discreet online communities and websites peddling racist disinformation.

In fact, for years one of the first websites about Martin Luther King Jr. that a Google search recommended was a website created by white nationalists that spread neo-Nazi propaganda.

In 2005, the white nationalist website Stormfront.org had 30,000 members—which might sound like a lot. But as social media expanded, with both Facebook and Twitter opening to anyone with an email address in 2006, its views got a lot more attention. By 2015, 250,000 people had subscribed to become members of Stormfront.org.

Between 2012 and 2016, white nationalists on Twitter saw a 600% increase in Twitter followers. They have since worked to bring white supremacism into everyday politics.

The Tech Transparency Project, a nonprofit tech industry watchdog group, found that in 2020 half of the white nationalist groups tracked by the Southern Poverty Law Center had a presence on Facebook.

Without clear regulations preventing extremist content, digital companies, in my view, allowed for the spread of white nationalist conspiracies.

Racist activists used algorithms as virtual bullhorns to reach previously unimaginable-sized audiences.

Enter the 'alt-right'

White nationalist leaders, such as Richard Spencer, wanted an even bigger audience and influence.

Spencer coined the term "alt-right" to this end, with the goal of blurring the relationship between white nationalism and white conservatism. He did this by establishing nonprofit think tanks like the National Policy Institute that provided an academic veneer for him and other white supremacists to spread their views on white supremacy.

This strategy worked.

Today, many white nationalist ideas once relegated to society's fringes are embraced by the broader conservative movement.

Take, for instance, the Great Replacement Theory. The conspiracy theory misinterprets demographic change as an active attempt to replace white Americans with people of color.

This baseless idea observes that Black and Latino people are becoming larger percentages of the U.S. population, and paints that data as the result of an allegedly active attempt by unnamed multiculturalists to drive white Americans out of power in an increasingly diverse nation.

A recent poll showed that over 50% of Republicans now believe in this conspiracy theory.

In 2016, during Trump's presidential campaign, *Vice Magazine* co-founder Gavin McInnes formed the Proud Boys to further the goals of the alt-right by protecting white identity with the use of violence if necessary.

Proud Boys members are affiliated with white nationalist ideas and leaders, but they deny any explicit racism. Instead, they describe themselves as "Western chauvinists" who believe in the supremacy of European culture but also welcome members of any race who support this idea.

Along with pro-gun militias such as the Oath Keepers and Three Percenters, the Proud Boys are an experiment in spreading white nationalist ideas to an online universe of potentially millions of social media users.

Why do people join these groups?

Data from manifestos posted online by white nationalist groups shows that many mass shooters share a few common characteristics–they are young, white, male and they spend significant time online at the same websites.

The alleged shooter in the killing of 10 Black people in a predominantly Black neighborhood in Buffalo on May 14, 2022, described his reason as wanting to stop what he feared as the elimination "of the white race."

His fears that people of color were "replacing" white people came from 4chan, a social media company popular among the alt-right.

In 2019, nine African American church members were murdered in Charleston by a young white man who became radicalized through Google searches that led him to openly white supremacist content.

Massacres in a Walmart in El Paso, Texas, at two mosques in Christchurch, New Zealand, and at a synagogue in Poway, California, all took place after the shooters began spending time on 8chan, an imageboard popular with white supremacists and the home of QAnon posts.

For many of these individuals, the most important part of their radicalization was not about their home life or personality quirks, but instead about where they spent time online.

A racially diverse democracy at stake

The reasons men join groups like the Proud Boys and Oath Keepers—and even some liberal groups—is less clear.

The Problems of Hate Speech

Hate speech is a complex and multidimensional phenomenon that has far-reaching and dangerous consequences for human rights, rule of law in democratic societies. Preventing and combating online hate speech poses specific challenges. The persistence and impact have been documented by the monitoring bodies of the Council of Europe and other international agencies.

Hate speech not only affects the dignity and human rights of the individual directly targeted, but also of persons belonging to the same minority or group as those directly targeted. Hate speech leads to dangerous divisions in society as a whole, affects the participation and inclusion of all those targeted by it and threatens democracy. The targets of hate speech become increasingly excluded from society, forced out of the public debate and silenced. History shows that hate speech has also been intentionally used to mobilise groups and societies against each other in order to provoke violent escalation, hate crime, war and genocide.

In recent years, hate speech has increasingly been spread through the internet. Preventing and combating online hate speech poses specific challenges, as it can be disseminated as never before across the world in a matter of seconds.

The persistence and worrying increase of hate speech, especially online, and its impact on the enjoyment of human rights and democracy in Europe have been documented by the monitoring bodies of the Council of Europe, the European Union Agency for Fundamental Rights (FRA), various other intergovernmental organisations, civil society organisations, internet intermediaries, and other bodies.

In its recent country monitoring and annual reports, the European Commission against Racism and Intolerance (ECRI) describes, based on detailed statistics and studies, the persistence and increase of ultra-nationalistic, xenophobic, racist, and LGBTI-phobic hate speech in various member States.

To avoid such dangerous escalation and rather establish and maintain inclusive societies, it is important that member States take effective and sustainable measures to prevent and combat hate speech.

"What is hate speech and why is it a problem?" by Council of Europe.

A former Proud Boy member offered one reason: "They want to join a gang," Russell Schultz told CNN on Nov. 25, 2020. "So they can go fight antifa and hurt people that they don't like, and feel justified in doing it."

Antifa is a loose-knit group of usually nonviolent activists who oppose fascism.

Other former extremist group members describe seeking camaraderie and friendship, but also finding racism and antisemitism.

But more than any other issue, racial demographic changes are providing recruitment opportunities for white nationalists, many of whom believe that by the year 2045 white people will become the minority in the United States.

In July 2021, the most recent date for which statistics are available, the U.S. Census Bureau notes that of the estimated population of 330 million American citizens, 75.8% are white, 18.9% are Hispanic, 13.6% are Black and 6% are Asian.

What is also becoming clearer is that the spread of white nationalism endangers the idea of a democratic nation where racial diversity is considered a strength, not a weakness.

Viewpoint 2

> *"In 2020 ... the population of Springfield was about 60,000. But over the past three years, city officials estimate that the population has grown by about 25%, partly fueled by the arrival of as many as 15,000 Haitian immigrants during that time."*

Recent Rapid Racial Change is Happening in Some US Cities

Paul J. Becker and Art Jipson

In the following viewpoint, Paul J. Becker and Art Jipson outline the activities of white supremacists and militia groups in Ohio. Paul J. Becker and Art Jipson are associate professors of sociology at the University of Dayton. Becker specializes in criminology and has been conducting research into right-wing extremism and hate groups for over 30 years. Jipson conducts research into cybercrime and extremism, and his work has been published in many academic criminal justice journals.

As you read, consider the following questions:

1. What do white extremists believe will happen soon, according to Becker and Jipson?

2. According to the authors, how do white supremacist and militia groups recruit members?
3. As stated by the examples of the viewpoint, which German social group do some white supremacists identify with?

The first time many Americans heard about Springfield, Ohio, came during the September 2024 presidential debate when Donald Trump falsely claimed that Haitian immigrants in the city were eating other residents' cats and dogs.

Though shocking, these harmful rumors had been spreading on social media since the beginning of the summer and had gained more notoriety when JD Vance, a U.S. senator from Ohio and Trump's running mate, made similar statements on X, the social media platform formerly called Twitter.

But what has gone mostly overlooked is the effect these racist lies have had on energizing Ohio's nearly 50 white extremist groups.

Members of the white supremacist group Blood Tribe marched through Springfield on Aug. 10, 2024, with swastikas on their signs.

Since then, members of the Ku Klux Klan and the right-wing extremist group Proud Boys have each marched in separate demonstrations through Springfield.

As scholars of extremism who live in Ohio and work at the University of Dayton, we have seen these events unfold at a time when city officials have received multiple bomb threats targeting local government offices and schools since Trump's false and racist claims against Haitian immigrants.

The changing landscape

In our research, we have found that the rapidly changing social conditions in Ohio have played a significant role in the growth of extremism.

Between 1990 and 2019, for instance, manufacturing jobs shrank from 21.7% of all employment in the state to 12.5%, a loss of nearly 360,000 jobs. As a result, income disparities between the professional and working classes have widened—as has the heightened sense among some alienated white men that white conservatives are the real victims of bias in a society growing more racially and culturally diverse.

For many of these alienated men, particularly those in rural areas that lack significant numbers of Black and Hispanic residents, extremist ideologies offer easy answers to complex questions that involve their sense of disenfranchisement.

In 2020, for example, the population of Springfield was about 60,000. But over the past three years, city officials estimate that the population has grown by about 25%, partly fueled by the arrival of as many as 15,000 Haitian immigrants during that time. Many of them are legally living in the U.S. under a special federal program.

Similar demographic shifts are occurring throughout the state. Between 2010 and 2022, the percentage of the white population dropped from 81.2% to 77.3%, a loss of about 250,000, putting the state's white population at about 9.1 million. During the same time, the Hispanic population, for instance, grew from about 357,000 in 2010 to nearly 525,000.

For some of these white extremists, these population changes will lead to an inevitable race war between white people and nonwhite people. We have found that the attraction of belonging to a group that promises strength, protection and a source of identity can be particularly compelling.

The Ohio connection

In recent years, white extremism in Ohio has received attention as a result of the extremist rhetoric of and often violent crimes committed by white men who call the state home. Consider just a few examples:

Born and raised in Ohio, Andrew Anglin founded the Daily Stormer, a popular neo-Nazi website, in 2016.

James Alex Fields Jr., a white nationalist from the Toledo area, was sentenced to life in prison in 2019 for the murder of

Heather Heyer in Charlottesville, Virginia. Fields was convicted of driving his car into a crowd of counterprotesters during the white nationalist Unite the Right Rally in August 2017.

Prior to the attack, Fields frequently posted the hashtag #Hitlerwasright on his social media accounts and called for violence against nonwhites and Jews.

In the summer of 2022, Ohio law enforcement officers shot and killed Ricky Shiffer after the armed Navy veteran fired a nail gun at the FBI field office in Cincinnati. On his social media accounts, Shiffer had called for violence against federal law enforcement officials after the FBI searched Donald Trump's residence at Mar-a-Lago as part of the federal probe into Trump's handling of classified documents.

Tres Genco, a self-described incel—short for "involuntary celibate"—who hated women and believed he was owed sex from them, was from the Cincinnati area and pled guilty in 2022 to plotting a mass shooting of women at Ohio State University. Law enforcement officials in Ohio stopped the planned attack before it happened.

On April 21, 2023, Christopher Brenner Cook, 20, of Columbus, Ohio, and others were sentenced to nearly eight years in prison for his plan to attack power grids across the U.S. Cook and his accomplices believed that they were starting a race war and used neo-Nazi propaganda and white supremacist ideology to recruit young people to join their group.

Online recruitment tactics

Leaders of white supremacist and militia groups often use both traditional outreach and digital platforms to recruit people to their groups. Traditional outreach includes recruitment in conversations, attending events, and sharing books, pamphlets, flyers and posters.

At the same time, social media has become a critical tool for extremist groups to spread their message, recruit members and organize events.

Hate Speech Leads to Violence

Hate speech covers many forms of expressions which advocate, incite, promote or justify hatred, violence and discrimination against a person or group of persons for a variety of reasons.

It poses grave dangers for the cohesion of a democratic society, the protection of human rights and the rule of law. If left unaddressed, it can lead to acts of violence and conflict on a wider scale. In this sense hate speech is an extreme form of intolerance which contributes to hate crime.

Aware of the dangerous link between hate speech and violence, ECRI has always considered that criminal prohibition is necessary when hate speech publicly incites violence against individuals or groups of people. At the same time criminal sanctions should be used as a measure of last resort and, all along, a balance must be kept between fighting hate speech on the one hand, and safeguarding freedom of speech on the other. Any restrictions on hate speech should not be misused to silence minorities and to suppress criticism of official policies, political opposition or religious beliefs.

In many instances, ECRI has found that an effective approach to tackling hate speech, in particular cyberhate, is self-regulation by

These online platforms create echo chambers that reinforce extremist beliefs in debunked conspiracy theories, such as the assumption that the federal government is part of a plot to eliminate the white race.

In addition to the increased traffic on social media, we have seen a rise of extremist groups in Ohio known as active clubs, where members engage in physical fitness, combat training and emotional support that encourages the development of a warrior mentality in preparation for what followers believe is an inevitable race war.

public and private institutions, media and the Internet industry, such as the adoption of codes of conduct accompanied by sanctions for non-compliance. Education and counter-speech are also equally important in fighting the misconceptions and misinformation that form the basis of hate speech. Therefore, ECRI considers that effective action against the use of hate speech requires raising public awareness of the importance of respecting pluralism and of the dangers posed by hate speech.

Underreporting of hate speech and hate-motivated violence is another unfortunate feature of these two phenomena. Victims rarely report incidents to the authorities for fear of retaliation or of not being taken seriously, or because they have no confidence in the justice system. This contributes to lack data which makes it difficult to quantify the extent of the problem and take effective measures to address it. ECRI recommends states to provide practical support to those targeted by hate speech and violence: they should be made aware of their rights to redress through administrative, civil and criminal proceedings and encouraged to report to the authorities, and receive legal and psychological assistance.

"Hate speech and violence" by Council of Europe.

Countering extremism in Ohio

Though the emergence of white extremist groups goes far beyond the borders of Ohio, we have found that community-based, educational initiatives are effective in understanding and ultimately eradicating the root causes of racial and ethnic hatred on the local level.

In our view, community engagement that emphasizes dialogue and understanding across different racial groups is crucial for demonstrating the dangers of intolerance—and the benefits of diversity.

Viewpoint 3

> *"A prominent US civil rights group, the Southern Poverty Law Center (SPLC) says that it is currently tracking more than 1,600 extremist groups in the country."*

Far-Right Groups are On the Rise in the US

The BBC

In the following viewpoint, the BBC maintains that alt-right groups in the US are increasing in numbers and membership with the election of Donald Trump to the White House. The BBC analyzes two of the most visible alt-right groups in the US and contends that their influence is growing. The BBC, British Broadcasting Service, is a news outlet in the UK.

As you read, consider the following questions:

1. As stated by the BBC, what do the alt-right groups use to boost their cause?
2. What are the two most visible alt-right groups in the US, according to the viewpoint?
3. Which alt-right group was formed after the Civil War, according to the author?

The deadly violence on the streets of Charlottesville, Virginia, comes at a time of a dramatic rise in prominence of far-right movements in the US.

The election of Donald Trump to the White House has been cited as a factor in the re-energization of activists and groups in America that reject both left-wing ideology and mainstream conservatism.

Social media is also said to be playing a large part in promoting these ideologies.

A prominent US civil rights group, the Southern Poverty Law Center (SPLC) says that it is currently tracking more than 1,600 extremist groups in the country.

But who are these groups, how popular have they become, and what do they hope to achieve?

Here is a look at the most visible of the white supremacist movements in the US today.

Alternative right (alt-right)

The alternative right (or alt-right) is a disparate group of provocateurs who hate political correctness and love Mr Trump, although critics say they are bigoted white nationalists.

This movement's recent rise is said to have been encouraged in part by the rhetoric employed during the 2016 US presidential election campaign, in which Mr Trump was accused of "textbook racism", anti-Semitism, and anti-Muslim bigotry.

Mr Trump, for his part, denounced the movement in November 2016, saying he disavowed their views.

The phrase "alt-right" started to gain traction in the mainstream media when Mr Trump, as then Republican nominee in July 2016, tweeted an image of Hillary Clinton alongside a six-pointed star resembling the Star of Israel containing the words: "Most Corrupt Candidate Ever!".

Alt-right factions, according to a guide written by Breitbart's Allum Bokhari and Milo Yiannopoulos, include "intellectuals", "natural conservatives" and "the meme team"—mostly young activists with a penchant for internet trolling.

The movement's ideals focus on "white identity" and the preservation of "traditional western civilisation", according to Richard Bertrand Spencer, who coined the term "alternative right" in 2008.

Liberty, free speech and the right to offend are its touchstones. Opponents call it racist, misogynist and anti-Semitic.

Number of members As a predominantly online movement, the alt-right does not officially have membership, therefore exact numbers are hard to come by.

Where are they? The presence of this "amorphous" movement is online and its popularity is said to be increasing nationwide.

Are they growing? A relatively new political movement, the group has gained increased prominence over the past year due to its enthusiastic support for Mr Trump. However estimating its strength is difficult.

Ku Klux Klan (KKK)

America's most infamous supremacist group, the initial KKK was formed by ex-Confederate officers in the southern states of the US in the aftermath of the American Civil War in 1865.

The Klan soon flourished in the south before spreading nationwide in the 1900s.

Divisions of the group discriminate against black Americans, Jews and immigrants, and more recently gays and lesbians.

It became a vigilante movement with the aim of preventing these groups from enjoying the same civil liberties and rights as their fellow Americans.

Members historically wore hooded costumes and carried out lynchings and other violent attacks on those challenging white supremacy in the southern states.

Factions of the group describe it as a "White Patriotic Christian organization that bases its roots back to the Ku Klux Klan of the early 20th century".

Number of members Klan groups are active in most US states and are estimated to have between 5,000 and 8,000 members, according to the SPLC.

Where are they? There are dozens of KKK groups in the US stretching from New Jersey to Los Angeles. Groups include the Confederate White Knights and the Traditionalist American Knights.

Are they growing? In 2016 the Klan said that it was in the midst of a revival with a "surge in membership across the Deep South".

Neo-Nazi groups

The term neo-Nazi relates to a group of separatist activists who share anti-Semitic ideals and a love for Adolf Hitler and Nazi Germany.

The views of neo-Nazi groups in the US are protected by the courts and the nation's First Amendment.

In one well-known case, the Supreme Court invoked the First Amendment to uphold the right of a neo-Nazi group to march through the predominantly Jewish town of Skokie, Illinois, and display swastikas.

Number of members There are several high-profile neo-Nazi organisations in the US, including the American Nazi Party and the National Socialist Movement (NSM). The most visible of these groups is the National Alliance (NA). A spin-off of the NA, Vanguard America, participated in the "Unite the Right" march on 12 August 2017 that left one woman dead and dozens of protesters and counter-protesters injured following clashes. The most recent membership figures for the NA, for 2012, are estimated to be at least 2,500, while an article published in the New York Times in 2011 said that the NSM consisted of about 400 members.

Where are they? A number of these groups were formed or originally based in Virginia. They have become more widespread in recent years with members of groups such as the NSM active in 32 states.

Are they growing? The manipulation of the mainstream media is attributed to a rise the far-right neo-Nazi movement, according to the Data and Society Research Institute. Links between US and European neo-Nazis are also said to be growing stronger, according to the SPLC.

Other white hate groups

National Socialist Movement: Founded in 1994, it is one of the largest neo-Nazi groups in the US, with chapters in more than 30 states.

Council of Conservative Citizens: Founded 1985, sprung from the pro-segregation movement in the southern states.

American Freedom Party: Founded 2009, with origins in California. Has a racist agenda and is against immigration.

Viewpoint 4

> *"Gypsy, Roma and Traveller communities continue to experience open discrimination and prejudice, both in the UK and Europe."*

Racism Against Roma, Gypsy, and Traveller Communities Continues and Worsens

Philip Brown

In the following viewpoint, Philip Brown argues that racism and ill treatment of Roma, Gypsy, and Traveller communities continues and is increasing with the increased population of such groups in the UK. Brown contends that Roma, Gypsy, and Traveller people suffer experiences and personal disabilities because of the adverse conditions they face in the countries in which they try to settle. The viewpoint argues that the UK must act to change. Philip Brown is a professor of social change at the University of Salford in the UK. The professor specializes in issues of migration and homelessness.

As you read, consider the following questions:

1. What is the purpose of International Roma Day, according to Brown?
2. Where are populations of Roma migrating to, as stated by the author?

3. What negative effects do Roma, Gypsy, and Traveller communities suffer as reported by the viewpoint?

Gypsy, Roma and Traveller communities continue to experience open discrimination and prejudice, both in the UK and Europe. Just in the past few weeks Roma people have been attacked in France as a result of fake news spread about the community. Meanwhile in the UK, the Equality and Human Rights Commission intervened in a holiday park which held a "no Travellers" rule, and a caravan site allocated for use for Travellers was subject to an arson attack.

April 8, 2019 marks International Roma Day—a day created to celebrate Romani culture and raise awareness of the issues facing Roma people. The day was established in 1990, but since this time the challenges Roma face have remained and even increased, driven by the rise of the Far Right and austerity.

The reality of their situation has been driven home by a new report from the House of Commons Women and Equalities Committee, which provides a damning critique of the progress made on addressing the inequalities faced by Gypsy, Roma and Traveller communities. It also challenges the government to do more to improve communities' outcomes in education and health care, tackle discrimination and hate crime, as well as violence against women and girls.

The committee report demands that the government develop a clear and effective plan to support Gypsy, Roma and Traveller communities, in line with the inequalities they face. The report also suggests a key role can be played by the Race Disparity Unit, which gathers information on the experiences of minority groups in the UK, by demanding that government departments must "explain or change" any disparities between Gypsy, Roma and Traveller communities and the general population.

A history of neglect

The fact is, the discrimination and adverse life chances faced by Gypsy, Roma and Traveller populations in the UK and Europe have been a problem for decades. Reports from the Commission for Racial Equality (in 2006), the Equality and Human Rights Commission (in 2010) and the European Commission (in 2018) have rigorously documented the inequalities and discrimination faced by these communities.

Indeed, the most recent of these confirmed that countries with larger Roma populations experienced an increase in anti-Roma hate speech, segregated and poor accommodation, even as hundreds of thousands of Roma endured a lack of access to basic services including clean water and sanitation. With the steady arrival of Roma from central and eastern Europe to the UK, there's a real risk of replicating the hostile anti-Roma environment seen in much of central and eastern Europe, which forces such communities to flee and polarises neighbourhoods.

The UK government's record on Roma issues has been one of inaction and neglect. Plans such as the coalition's 2012 strategy to tackle inequalities have been widely derided for having limited scope, little ambition and weak recommendations. The most recent inquiry failed to consider the shortage of pitches and site accommodation across the UK, which many groups representing Roma, Gypsy and Traveller communities would consider to be one of the most pressing concerns.

Yet the report represents a significant intervention against government inaction and hostile policy making. Few politicians—with notable exceptions such as Kate Green and Baronness Whitaker—speak out against the inequalities faced by Gypsy, Roma and Traveller communities. Indeed, during the inquiry, Conservative MP Jackie Doyle-Price said: "Let's be honest: we are all Members of Parliament and we all know there are no votes in championing this group of people".

As with all reports prepared by parliamentary committees, the government has 40 days to respond. With the current atmosphere of anti-migrant sentiment in the UK, coupled with the continuing hostility to Gypsies and Travellers, it is difficult to predict the sort of response the report will receive. But maintaining the status quo cannot be an option.

Turning point

Gypsy, Roma and Traveller communities, on average, continue to die far younger than members of other communities and have poorer health than members of other communities. They also experience the death of a child far frequently than other communities. The needs and position of Gypsy, Roma and Traveller communities are so stark that considered steps must be taken.

So this should be an opportunity for the government and other public bodies to take more forceful and co-ordinated action. One way forward is for the government to use the Race Disparity Audit to address inequalities. Vocal leadership is also required from within government at all levels. For too long, Gypsy, Roma and Traveller communities have been used as a political football, with few people in positions of power speaking up for their needs.

Successive governments have tried doing nothing, pilot projects have been attempted and mainstreaming the needs of Gypsy, Roma and Traveller communities has been the recent approach. But all have failed over the long term or led to very little improvement. Government needs to lead and to foster leadership in others—there needs to be coordinated plans and actions. As in most areas, resources will also be an issue, but a desire and an ability to affect change is critical. In doing so, the UK will address some of the longstanding issues for Gypsy, Roma and Traveller people and make communities more equal and less hostile places.

VIEWPOINT 5

> *"Antisemitism has been called history's oldest hatred ... Understood this way, it is the modern manifestation of an ancient prejudice—one which some scholars believe stretches back to antiquity and medieval times."*

Antisemitism Is History's Oldest Hatred

Gervase Phillips

In the following viewpoint, Gervase Phillips argues that antisemitism is history's oldest hatred, stretching back to medieval times. Phillips analyzes the hatred for Jews in history, and then draws similarities to this hatred that has morphed into today's society and cultural incidents. Gervase Phillips is a lecturer in history at the Manchester Metropolitan University in the UK. He is dedicated to the study and teaching of history and his research centers on human conflict.

As you read, consider the following questions:

1. According to the viewpoint, what is causing a resurgence of antisemitism?
2. As stated by the author, what caused hatred against Jews in antiquity?

"Antisemitism: how the origins of history's oldest hatred still hold sway today" by Gervase Phillips, *The Conversation*, February 27, 2018.

3. How does white supremacy interact with the Civil War, according to Phillips?

Antisemitism is on the march. From the far-right demonstrators in Charlottesville, Virginia, with their "Blood and Soil" chants and their "Jews will not replace us" placards to attacks on synagogues in Sweden, arson attacks on kosher restaurants in France and a spike in hate crimes against Jews in the UK. Antisemitism seems to have been given a new lease of life.

The seemingly endless conflicts in the Middle East have made the problem worse as they spawn divisive domestic politics in the West. But can the advance of antisemitism be attributed to the rise of right-wing populism or the influence of Islamic fundamentalism? One thing is clear. Antisemitism is here and it's getting worse.

Antisemitism rears its ugly head in every aspect of public life, whether internal debates within political parties or accusations of conspiratorial networks or plots in politics and business. Or even in the accusations that Hollywood mogul Harvey Weinstein's sexually predatory behaviour was somehow linked to his Jewish origins.

But by focusing narrowly on the contemporary context of modern antisemitism, we miss a central, if deeply depressing, reality. Jeffrey Goldberg, the editor of *The Atlantic* magazine, puts it correctly when he says that what we are seeing is an ancient and deeply embedded hostility towards Jews that is reemerging as the barbarous events of World War II recede from our collective memory.

Goldberg says that for 70 years, in the shadow of the death camps, antisemitism was culturally, politically and intellectually unacceptable. But now "we are witnessing … the denouement of an unusual epoch in European life, the age of the post-Holocaust Jewish dispensation". Without an understanding of antisemitism's ancient roots, the dark significance of this current trend may not be fully understood and hatred may sway popular opinion unchallenged.

Antisemitism has been called history's oldest hatred and it has shown itself to be remarkably adaptable. It is carved from—and sustained by—powerful precedents and inherited stereotypes. But it also taking on variant forms to reflect the contingent fears and anxieties of an ever-changing world. Understood this way, it is the modern manifestation of an ancient prejudice—one which some scholars believe stretches back to antiquity and medieval times.

Ancient tradition of hatred

The word "antisemitism" was popularised by the German journalist Wilhelm Marr. His polemic, *Der Sieg des Judentums über das Germentum* (*The Victory of Jewry over Germandom*), was published in 1879. Outwardly, Marr was a thoroughly secular man of the modern world. He explicitly rejected the groundless but ancient Christian allegations long made against the Jews, such as deicide or that Jews engaged in the ritual murder of Christian children. Instead, he drew on the fashionable theories of the French academic Ernest Renan (who viewed history as a world-shaping contest between Jewish Semites and Aryan Indo-Europeans). Marr suggested that the Jewish threat to Germany was racial. He said that it was born of their immutable and destructive nature, their "tribal peculiarities" and "alien essence".

Antisemites like Marr strove for intellectual respectability by denying any connection between their own modern, secular ideology and the irrational, superstitious bigotry of the past. It is a tactic which is employed by some contemporary antisemites who align themselves with "anti-Zionism", an ideology whose precise definition consequently excites considerable controversy. But this continuing hostility towards Jews from pre-modern to modern times has been manifest to many.

The American historian Joshua Trachtenberg, writing during World War II, noted:

> *Modern so-called 'scientific' antisemitism is not an invention of Hitler's ... it has flourished primarily in central and eastern Europe, where medieval ideas and conditions have persisted until this day, and where the medieval conception of the Jew which underlies the prevailing emotional antipathy toward him was, and still is, deeply rooted.*

In fact, up until the Holocaust, antisemitism flourished just as much in western Europe as in central or eastern Europe. Consider, for example, how French society was bitterly divided between 1894-1906, after the Jewish army officer, Captain Alfred Dreyfus, was falsely accused and convicted of spying for Germany. It saw conservatives squaring up against liberals and socialists, Catholics against Jews.

Yet Trachtenberg was undoubtedly correct in suggesting that many of those who shaped modern antisemitism were profoundly influenced by the older "medieval" tradition of religious bigotry. The Russian editor of the infamous Protocols of Zion—a crude and ugly, but tragically influential, forgery alleging a Jewish world conspiracy—was the political reactionary, ultra-Orthodox, and self-styled mystic Sergei Nilus.

Wrought by fear and hatred of the challenges to traditional religion, social hierarchies and culture posed by modernity, Nilus was convinced that the coming of the Antichrist was imminent and that those who failed to believe in the existence of "the elders of Zion" were simply the dupes of "Satan's greatest ruse".

So modern antisemitism cannot be easily separated from its pre-modern antecedents. As the Catholic theologian Rosemary Ruether observed:

> *The mythical Jew, who is the eternal conspiratorial enemy of Christian faith, spirituality and redemption, was ... shaped to serve as the scapegoat for [the ills of] secular industrial society.*

Antisemitism in antiquity?

Some scholars would look to the pre-Christian world and see in the attitudes of ancient Greeks and Romans the origins of an enduring hostility. Religious Studies scholar Peter Schäfer believes the exclusive nature of the monotheistic Jewish faith, the apparent haughty sense of being a chosen people, a refusal to intermarry, a Sabbath observance and the practise of circumcision were all things that marked Jews out in antiquity for a particular odium.

Finding examples of hostility towards Jews in classical sources is not difficult. The politician and lawyer Cicero, 106-43BC, once reminded a jury of "the odium of Jewish gold" and how they "[stick together]" and are "influential in informal assemblies". The Roman historian Tacitus, c.56-120AD, was contemptuous of "base and abominable" Jewish customs and was deeply disturbed by those of his compatriots who had renounced their ancestral gods and converted to Judaism. The Roman poet and satirist Juvenal, c.55-130AD, shared his disgust at the behaviour of converts to Judaism besides denouncing Jews generally as drunken and rowdy.

These few examples may point towards the existence of antisemitism in antiquity. But there is little reason to believe that Jews were the objects of a specific prejudice beyond the generalised contempt that both Greeks and Romans exhibited towards "barbarians"—especially conquered and colonised peoples. Juvenal was every bit as rude about Greeks and other foreigners in Rome as he was about Jews. He complained bitterly: "I cannot stand … a Greek city of Rome. And yet what part of the dregs comes from Greece?" Once the full extent of Juvenal's prejudice has been recognised, his snide remarks about Jews might be understood as being more indicative of an altogether more sweeping xenophobia.

The 'Christ killers'

It is in the theology of early Christians that we find the clearest foundations of antisemitism. The Adversus Judaeos (arguments against the Jews) tradition was established early in the religion's history. Sometime around 140AD the Christian apologist Justin Martyr was teaching in Rome. In his most celebrated work, *Dialogue with Trypho the Jew*, Justin strove to answer Trypho when he pointed to the contradictory position of Christians who claimed to accept Jewish scripture but refused to follow Torah (the Jewish law).

Justin responded that the demands of Jewish law were meant only for Jews as a punishment from God. Although still accepting the possibility of Jewish salvation, he argued that the old covenant was finished, telling Trypho: "You ought to understand that [the gifts of God's favour] formerly among your nation have been transferred to us." Yet Justin's concern was not really with Jews. It was with his fellow Christians. At a time when the distinction between Judaism and Christianity was still blurred and rival sects competed for adherents, he was striving to prevent gentile converts to Christianity from observing the Torah, lest they go over wholly to Judaism.

Vilifying Jews was a central part of Justin's rhetorical strategy. He alleged that they were guilty of persecuting Christians and had done so ever since they "had killed the Christ". It was an ugly charge, soon levelled again in the works of other Church Fathers, such as Tertullian (c.160-225AD) who referred to the "synagogues of the Jews" as "fountains of persecution".

The objective of using such invective was to settle internal debates within Christian congregations. The "Jews" in these writings were symbolic. The allegations did not reflect the actual behaviour or beliefs of Jews. When Tertullian attempted to refute the dualist teachings of the Christian heretic Marcion (c.144 AD), he needed to demonstrate that the vengeful God of the Old Testament was indeed the same merciful and compassionate God of the Christian New Testament. He achieved this by presenting the Jews as especially wicked and especially deserving of righteous anger; it was thus, Tertullian argued, that Jewish behaviours and Jewish sins explained the contrast between the Old and the New Testament.

To demonstrate this peculiar malevolence, Tertullian portrayed Jews as denying the prophets, rejecting Jesus, persecuting Christians and as rebels against God. These stereotypes shaped Christian attitudes towards Jews from late antiquity into the medieval period, leaving Jewish communities vulnerable to periodic outbreaks of persecution. These ranged from massacres, such as York in 1190, to "ethnic cleansing", as seen in the expulsions from England in 1290, France in 1306 and Spain in 1492.

Although it was real people who often suffered as a result of this ugly prejudice, antisemitism as a concept largely owes its longevity to its symbolic and rhetorical power. American historian David Nirenberg concludes that "anti-Judaism was a tool that could usefully be deployed to almost any problem, a weapon that could be deployed on almost any front". And this weapon has been wielded to devastating effect for centuries. When Martin Luther thundered against the Papacy in 1543 he denounced the Roman Church as "the Devil's Synagogue" and Catholic orthodoxy as "Jewish" in its greed and materialism. In 1790, the Anglo-Irish conservative Edmund Burke published his manifesto, Reflections on the Revolution in France, and condemned the revolutionaries as "Jew brokers" and "Old Jewry."

From Marxism to Hollywood

Despite Karl Marx's Jewish ancestry, Marxism was tainted at its very birth by antisemitism. In 1843, Karl Marx identified modern capitalism as the result of the "Judiasing" of the Christian:

> *The Jew has emancipated himself in a Jewish manner not only annexing the power of money but also through him and also apart from him money has become a world power and the practical spirit of the Jew has become the practical spirit of the Christian people. The Jews have emancipated themselves in so far as the Christians have become Jews ... Money is the jealous god of Israel before whom no other god may stand ... The god of the Jews has been secularised and has become the god of the world.*

And there remain those, from across the political spectrum, who are still ready to deploy what Nirenberg referred to as "the most powerful language of opprobrium available" in Western political discourse, commonly using the language of conspiracy, webs and networks. In 2002, the left-leaning New Statesman included articles by Dennis Sewell and John Pilger, debating the existence of a "pro-Israeli lobby" in Britain. Their articles, however, proved less controversial than the the cover illustration chosen to introduce this theme, which drew on familiar tropes of secret

Jewish machinations and dominance over national interests: a gold Star of David resting on the Union Jack, with the title: "A Kosher Conspiracy?" The following year, veteran Labour MP Tam Dalyell accused the then prime minister, Tony Blair, of "being unduly influenced by a cabal of Jewish advisers". It is still language that is being used now.

On the far right, white supremacists have been quick to project their own time-honoured fantasies of Jewish malfeasance and power onto contemporary events, however seemingly irrelevant. This was quickly apparent in August 2017, as the future of memorials glorifying those who had rebelled against the union and defended slavery during America's Civil War became the focus of intense debate in the United States. At Charlottesville, Virginia, demonstrators protesting against the removal of a statue of Confederate General Robert E Lee, began chanting "Jews will not replace us". When journalist Elspeth Reeve asked one why, he replied that the city was "run by Jewish communists".

When accusations of serious sexual misconduct by Weinstein were published by *The New York Times* in October 2017, he was quickly cast by the far right as a representative of the "eternal conspiratorial enemy" of American society as a whole. David Duke, former head of the Ku Klux Klan, would write on his website that the "Harvey Weinstein story … is a case study in the corrosive nature of Jewish domination of our media and cultural industries".

'The hatreds of our time …'

Responding to such language, *The Atlantic*'s Emma Green astutely commented on how "the durability of anti-Semitic tropes and the ease with which they slide into all displays of bigotry, is a chilling reminder that the hatreds of our time rhyme with history and are easily channelled through timeless anti-Semitic canards".

There is real danger here as the spike in antisemitic hate crimes shows. This peculiar way of thinking about the world has always retained the potential to turn hatred of symbolic Jews into the very real persecution of actual Jews. Given the marked escalation of antisemitic incidents recorded in 2017, we are now faced with the unsettling prospect that this bigotry is becoming "normalised".

For example, the European Jewish Congress expressed "grave concerns" over an increase in antisemitic acts in Poland under the right-wing Law and Justice government which won the 2015 parliamentary election with an outright majority. The group said the government was "closing … communications with the official representatives of the Jewish community" and there was a "proliferation of 'fascist slogans' and unsettling remarks on social media and television, as well as the display of flags of the nationalist … group at state ceremonies".

In response to these fears, a survey investigating antisemitism within the European Union will be undertaken in 2018, led by the European Union Agency for Fundamental Rights. The agency's director, Michael O'Flaherty, commented, correctly, that: "Antisemitism remains a grave worry across Europe despite repeated efforts to stamp out these age-old prejudices."

Given the phenomenon's deep historical roots and its epoch defying capacity for reinvention, it would be easy to be pessimistic about the prospect of another effort to "stamp it out". But an historical awareness of the nature of antisemitism may prove a powerful ally for those who would challenge prejudice. The ancient tropes and slights may cloak themselves in modern garb but even softly-spoken allegations of conspiratorial "lobbies" and "cabals" should be recognised for what they are: the mobilisation of an ancient language and ideology of hate for which there should be no place in our time.

Periodical and Internet Sources Bibliography

The following articles have been selected to supplement the diverse views presented in this chapter.

Audra D. S. Burch, "White Supremacist Incidents are Rising Across the U.S.," *The New York Times*, November 21, 2024. www.nytimes.com/2024/11/21/us/trump-neo-nazi-anti-government-groups.html.

Ashley Murray, "White nationalist, Anti-LGBTQ Activity on the Rise, Annual Hate Report Shows," *Missouri Independent*, June 5, 2024. missouriindependent.com/2024/06/05/white-nationalist-anti-lgbtq-activity-on-the-rise-annual-hate-report-shows/.

Simon Clark, "How White Supremacy Returned to Mainstream Politics," Center for American Progress, July 1, 2020. www.americanprogress.org/article/white-supremacy-returned-mainstream-politics/.

Luis Andres Henao, "Haitian Migrants in Springfield, Ohio, Turn to Faith Amid Deportation Fears," AP, January 27, 2025. apnews.com/article/trump-immigration-haitian-migrants-ohio-deportation-fears-c28786fcf3b9e4f99b576330e9fb87d1.

Wesley Lowery, "American Whitelash: Fear Mongering and the Rise in White Nationalist Violence," CBS, June 25, 2023. www.cbsnews.com/news/american-whitelash-fear-mongering-and-the-rise-in-white-nationalist-violence/.

Ben Makuch, "Energized Neo-Nazis Feel Their Moment Has Come as Trump Changes Everything," *The Guardian*, January 26, 2025. www.theguardian.com/us-news/2025/jan/26/neo-nazis-trump-extremism.

Bernard Rorke, "Italy: Inciting Hatred Against Romani Women," European Roma Rights Centre, November 24, 2023. www.errc.org/news/italy-inciting-hatred-against-romani-women.

Catherine E. Shoichet, "Why Springfield? How a Small Ohio City Became Home for Thousands of Haitians," CNN, September 19, 2024. www.cnn.com/2024/09/19/us/springfield-ohio-haitians-immigration-cec.

Haroon Siddique, "Gypsy, Roma, and Travellers Suffer Persistent Discrimination in UK," *The Guardian*, May 25, 2023.

www.theguardian.com/world/2023/may/25/gypsy-roma-travellers-suffer-persistent-discrimination-uk.

Judy Woodruff, "How Springfield and Its Haitian Immigrants are Still Dealing with Election's Spotlight," PBS News, April 23, 2025. www.pbs.org/newshour/show/how-springfield-and-its-haitian-immigrants-are-still-dealing-with-elections-spotlight.

Odette Yousef, "Active Club Hate Groups are Growing in the U.S.- and Making Themselves Seen," NPR, July 9, 2023. www.npr.org/2023/07/19/1188111769/active-club-hate-groups.

OPPOSING VIEWPOINTS® SERIES

Chapter 2

How Does Politics Impact Hate Speech and Hate Groups?

Chapter Preface

At the present time, it may appear that many people disagree with one another so strongly that they cannot find common ground. Government officials, both local and national, are seen trading insults and unprofessional speech and accusations. Some people lament that Americans have become unable to tolerate differing opinions. However, research from the University of Notre Dame's Rooney Center for the Study of American Democracy in Notre Dame, Indiana, found that many Americans, regardless of political affiliation, agree on what to censor when it comes to hate speech.

The viewpoint articles in this chapter analyze the intersection of politics and hate speech. Several viewpoints focus on the effects of the Israeli-Hamas war and how this global conflict affects hate speech around the country. It's not difficult to imagine the spillover onto college campuses that has occurred since this war began. Another viewpoint author stresses that violence increases when polarizing speech, especially from politicians, increases. This effect has been seen in the United States and elsewhere around the world.

Two viewpoints shed light on the individuals and groups that use hate speech to their political advantage, and one viewpoint analyzes how a once well-known racist politician actually changed his actions and speech because of a personal experience.

Viewpoint 1

> *"How can the twice-impeached, twice indicted election denier who incited the attack on the Capitol, was convicted of sexual assault, and is still the subject of numerous judicial investigations—including for election interference—still dominate the Republican Party?"*

Donald Trump Remains Popular with Republican Voters

Jerome Viala-Gaudefroy

In the following viewpoint, Jerome Viala-Gaudefroy analyzes the popularity among Republican voters for Donald Trump. Viala-Gaudefroy contends that there is a certain base of voters that support Trump seemingly because of his anti-elite, anti-education, and racist attitudes. Jerome Viala-Gaudefroy is an assistant lecturer in contemporary American politics in Paris.

As you read, consider the following questions:

1. According to the viewpoint, do Trump supporters still believe that the 2020 election was stolen?

2. Which population group makes up Trump supporters, as reported by this viewpoint?
3. What fears propel Trump voters to back their candidate, according to the author?

Donald Trump has once again been indicted, this time at the federal level for violating the Espionage Act and endangering US security in his handling of classified documents. Unsurprisingly, he maintains his innocence, accusing the Biden administration of "election interference at the highest level" and "weaponization of the Justice Department and the FBI". This defense, echoed by Fox News, has also been adopted by leading members of the Republican party, including Kevin McCarthy, the Speaker of the House of Representatives.

Even his opponents in the primaries, starting with his main rival Ron Desantis, have almost universally embraced the narrative of an indictment that is purely a political attack by Joe Biden on one of the leading contenders for the Republican presidential nomination.

If the most prominent Republicans are either defending the former president or keeping a low profile, it's because Donald Trump remains very popular with right-wing voters. He leads the polls in primary voting intentions at over 50%, racing ahead over his main rival, Desantis, by more than 30 points. This gap continues to widen, even in the state of Florida, where Ron Desantis was overwhelmingly re-elected governor in 2022.

In line with previous scandals, the new indictment is unlikely to dent Republican voters' support for the former president. It could even strengthen it, especially since, if convicted, Trump would remain electable anyway. Indeed, under the Constitution and the 14th Amendment, only a conviction for insurrection or rebellion could disqualify him. Theoretically, he could campaign from prison, as another candidate, Eugene Debbs, did in 1920 and immediately pardon himself if elected.

How can the twice-impeached, twice indicted election denier who incited the attack on the Capitol, was convicted of sexual assault, and is still the subject of numerous judicial investigations—including for election interference—still dominate the Republican Party?

On paper, it would appear there is room for an alternative to Trump within the party, especially after the disappointing results for Republicans in the 2022 mid-term elections. In fact, despite appearances, the so-called "MAGA" (Make American Great Again) republicans are in the minority in the party. According to a study published in 2022, they represent around a third of the Republicans (30 to 37%), or roughly 15% of American voters, a number confirmed by a recent NBC poll.

Divided Republicans

The problem is that, apart from this homogeneous radicalized pro-Trump base unified around the former president, the Republicans are divided. Those who might be prepared to opt for a candidate other than the former president are motivated to varying degrees and for various reasons. And almost a third of them (i.e. 20% of Republican voters) have not found an alternative candidate and therefore say they are ready to rally behind Trump.

The challenge for any of Trump's competitors is not only to rally a sufficiently large percentage of Republican voters under the same banner but also to position themselves as both heir and rival to Donald Trump. Meanwhile, the former president will not pull his punches against anyone he might perceive as a threat, as he has been doing with Desantis.

What's more, he benefits from the proliferation of primary candidates. The first-past-the-post system used in the primaries and the fact that, in most states, the candidate with the highest number of votes wins all the delegates are likely to favour the former president who can rely on his solid electoral base.

Almost a dozen have already officially declared their candidacy. But none of them seem to be emerging yet, and, apart from former New Jersey Governor Chris Christie, and former Vice President

Mike Pence, who were already perceived as disloyal even before they entered the race, the primary candidates have largely avoided attacking Trump heads-on, preferring to save their blows for Desantis.

One other important factor not often considered is that only a tiny minority of voters cast a ballot in the primaries—less than 15% turnout among Republicans in 2016, which is still the highest rate in over 30 years. It is often assumed that it is the more radicalised fringe that votes in this poll, although research on this subject is inconclusive.

A more radical but less charismatic rival

The strategy adopted by Ron Desantis is to campaign to the right of Trump on cultural war themes: anti-woke, anti-abortion, anti-transgender and LGBT, and pro-gun. But in so doing, DeSantis is actually seeking to appeal to a segment of the electorate quite similar to that of Trump.

Described by the *Financial Times* as a "Donald Trump with brains and without the drama," he is also known for his lack of charisma. His style of governance in Florida is based on authoritarianism and the political weaponization of institutions, including schools. In this regard, he is more like Viktor Orbán than the former American president. What's more, having praised Donald Trump exceedingly, he now has to attack him without contradicting himself or, worse still, looking like a traitor to his base.

Racial resentment as a unifying factor

As soon as the former president is in trouble, a vast majority (70%) of Republican sympathizers rally behind him. For the majority of Republicans, the mere idea of an indictment feels politically motivated. Similarly, a majority continues to believe that the 2020 election was stolen from them, including those who now recognize that there is no proof whatsoever.

This enduring suspicion illustrates not only that perception counts for more than reality, but also that there is a form of paranoia symptomatic of an identity crisis rooted in economic anxiety and

Charlottesville car attack suspect charged with hate crime

An Ohio man accused of driving his car into a crowd of protesters in Virginia last year and killing a woman has been charged with federal hate crimes.

James Alex Fields Jr is already facing charges of murder and other crimes at the state level in Virginia. He has been held in jail without bail.

Prosecutors say he deliberately drove into a group of people who gathered to protest a white nationalist rally.

Graphic video of the incident was widely shared on social media.

Heather Heyer, 32, who was demonstrating against the 12 August event, was struck and killed and dozens of others were injured.

Mr Fields, 21, was charged on Wednesday with 29 counts of hate crime acts, including causing injury and involving an attempt to kill.

Federal prosecutors allege that Mr Fields thought about harming others while driving to Charlottesville last summer.

The indictment also found evidence on Fields' social media of the suspect "expressing support of the social and racial policies of Adolf Hitler and Nazi-era Germany, including the Holocaust".

He joined in on racist, anti-Semitic and white-supremacist chanting, and when the assembly was dispersed, he drove his car intentionally

racial resentment. Research has extensively documented that Donald Trump's voters are predominantly white, non-educated, evangelical and middle-class, and that it was primarily the question of identity—especially related to race, religion and gender—more than the economy, that was the driving force behind Trump's election in 2016.

For part of this white American electorate, this comes down to what sociologist Arlie Hochschild calls "a deep history". This story is that middle-class whites are ostracized by minority groups, abandoned by the government, victimized and treated with contempt by a left-wing elite. Their resentment stems in part from their weakening demographics: their share of the electorate fell from 69% in 1980 to 39% in 2020, and is expected to fall to 30% by 2032.

into a "racially and ethnically diverse crowd of individuals", according to the indictment.

In a statement, Attorney General Jeff Sessions said the Department of Justice remains "resolute that hateful ideologies will not have the last word".

"Last summer's violence in Charlottesville cut short a promising young life and shocked the nation," Mr Sessions said.

"Today's indictment should send a clear message to every would-be criminal in America that we aggressively prosecute violent crimes of hate that threaten the core principles of our nation."

Convicted criminals can face life in prison or the death penalty for hate crime-motivated murders, according to US hate crime laws.

The 2017 white supremacist rally that took place in Charlottesville, Virginia was one of the largest gathering of white nationalists in America in decades.

Dozens were injured in the violence that erupted between white nationalists and counter-protesters.

The "Unite the Right" march was organised to protest against plans to remove a statue of a general who had fought for the pro-slavery Confederacy during the US Civil War.

"Charlottesville car attack suspect charged with hate crime"by BBC, June 28, 2018.

Trump's "emotional strategy"

Donald Trump's success stems from his charisma and his ability to tap into the fear, resentment and humiliation of that deep story. Trump has his own resentment toward the New York elite, and toward successful Black men like Barack Obama who he sees as unqualified or guilty of stealing his success by polarizing American politics around the issue of race.

What's remarkable, and perhaps counter-intuitive, is that this narrative of racial resentment is even sometimes adopted by minorities who feel antipathy toward other minority groups. A recent study shows, for example, a growing number of Latinos and people of colour in the white supremacist movement.

Trump has also been able to tap into white evangelical Christians' fear, as Kristin Kobes Du Mez has shown, offering them a narrative of "American carnage" that resonates with their eschatological beliefs of decline and destruction in the end times.

Martyr and superhero

Donald Trump has built a narrative around himself in which he is a victim-in-chief, even a martyr, with whom his electorate can identify on the one hand and, and a hypemasculinized superhero in whom his base can project itself on the other. On the eve of the 2016 elections, he claimed to be the "voice of the forgotten". Ahead of the 2024 primaries, he presents himself as their "warrior" and "justice," promising to be the "retribution" for "those who have been wronged and betrayed."

That vengeance applies as well to the Republicans who betray him. Let's not forget that Kevin McCarthy, whose leadership of the House relies on a slim majority, is at the mercy of the most pro-Trump fringe of his party's elected representatives. In the same way, the Grand Old Party is held hostage by a powerful minority movement whose only consistency is its unquestioned loyalty to their leader, Donald Trump, even if it means weakening the party and losing elections.

In such a context, we can legitimately wonder what would happen if Trump were to lose the Republican primaries. It is not impossible that he would then reject the results and claim that they were rigged as he did in 2020. If he were to run then as an independent, almost 30% of Republican voters would be ready to follow him, even if history and research shows that he would have almost no chance of winning. In any case, he would blow up the Republican Party, a possibility that only strengthens his domination over an already weakened party, incapable of redefining itself along any clear ideological and intellectual lines.

Viewpoint 2

> *"At a recent rally, former President Donald Trump used language in a speech that echoed Adolf Hitler, comparing his political opponents to 'vermin.'"*

It Matters When Politicians Call Their Opponents Inappropriate Names

Danielle Kurtzleben

In the following viewpoint, Danielle Kurtzleben maintains that the language used by a country's leader can sway voters. Kurtzleben outlines how authoritarians use speech to rally supporters and make them believe that they are under attack. For this reason, Kurtzleben points out that authoritarians control the population and have them believe that there is an enemy within that needs to be eradicated or feared. Danielle Kurtzleben is a political correspondent for NPR. Kurtzleben covered the 2024 presidential election, and in her work, she specializes in gender politics and economic policy.

As you read, consider the following questions:

1. How is authoritarianism defined in the viewpoint?
2. What language does Trump use that makes him similar to Hitler, as stated by the viewpoint article?

"Why Trump's authoritarian language about 'vermin' matters" by Danielle Kurtzleben, November 17, 2023. National Public Radio Inc. (NPR). Reprinted by permission.

3. According to the viewpoint, how do authoritarians take root in a society?

At a recent rally, former President Donald Trump used language in a speech that echoed Adolf Hitler, comparing his political opponents to "vermin."

"We pledge to you that we will root out the communists, Marxists, fascists, and the radical left thugs that live like vermin within the confines of our country," he told a New Hampshire crowd.

There were other nods to authoritarianism in the speech. Trump praised Hungary's strongman leader: "The head of Hungary—very tough, strong guy—Viktor Orban," Trump told the audience, adding approvingly, "He didn't allow millions of people to invade his country."

Later on, Trump referred to himself as "a very proud election denier."

Authoritarian rhetoric has been central to Trump's political trajectory—and his time as president. Ruth Ben-Ghiat, professor of history at NYU and author of the book "Strongman," defines authoritarianism this way:

"It's when the executive branch and the leader find ways to take away checks and balances," she said. "So they have a degree of power that they don't have in a democracy, and they find ways to take away the independence of the legislature and the independence of the judiciary."

She points to a *New York Times* report that Trump is looking for potential appointees who will not stymie his attempts at greater executive power.

Authoritarianism, in fact, has been found to be key to Trump's political success. In a 2016 study, political scientist Matthew MacWilliams found that belief in authoritarian ideas was the greatest predictor of support for Trump in that Republican primary.

And even in America's heretofore stable democracy, authoritarianism is relatively popular—MacWilliams later found that around 4 in 10 Americans have authoritarian preferences.

"What we have witnessed from Trump over the last few weeks is something new," said Robert Jones, founder of the Public Religion Research Institute, or PRRI. "Trump has clearly crossed into the domain of Nazi ideology openly."

Jones also pointed to a recent interview with the far-right website The National Pulse, in which Trump said that immigration is "a very sad thing for our country; it's poisoning the blood of our country."

The Trump campaign firmly denies any connection to Nazi rhetoric. In a statement, spokesman Steven Cheung told NPR: "Everything President Trump is saying is true. It's honestly despicable and racist for any news organization to make disgusting connections as they have done in the past few days."

He added, "There has been no bigger ally to Israel and the Jewish people than President Trump."

Many people listening to his speech or that National Pulse interview might not realize that Trump's language echoes language Hitler used. But Jones argues that that's not the only reason Trump's language matters:

"This language of rooting out vermin—the reason why authoritarian leaders use that is because it does dehumanize their political opponents," he explained.

"The dehumanization of political opponents are the bricks that pave the road to political violence," Jones said.

PRRI recently found that 23 percent of voters, including one-third of Republicans, agreed that "true American patriots may have to resort to violence in order to save our country."

That poll also found that 38 percent of Americans, including nearly half of Republicans, agree that the U.S. needs a leader who "is willing to break some rules if that is what it takes to set things right." Jones sees this as a clear indication of authoritarian sentiment.

Othering an entire group, whether it's immigrants or political opponents, is powerful for authoritarians, says Ben-Ghiat.

"You need to get people to feel they have an existential threat facing them," she said. "And the more they feel uncertain and

Proud Boys and antifa—who are they and what do they want?

President Trump mentioned a far-right group during the first presidential debate, kicking off online celebrations by its supporters.

"Proud Boys—stand back and stand by," he said, in a response to a question asking him to condemn white supremacist and militia groups. Members of the group online took the answer as a call to prepare for action.

Mr Trump then insisted that violence was coming from far-left activists: "Somebody's got to do something about antifa and the left, because this is not a right-wing problem."

Joe Biden, the Democratic challenger, answered back: "Antifa is an idea, not an organisation. That is what [President Trump's] FBI director said."

Over the past few years, a number of fringe groups have been engaged in politically motivated violence on American streets. So who are Proud Boys and antifa?

Proud Boys

Founded in 2016 by Canadian-British right-wing activist Gavin McInnes, the Proud Boys is a far-right, anti-immigrant, all-male group with a history of street violence against its left-wing opponents.

The group's name is a reference to a song from the musical version of the Disney film *Aladdin*. Members often wear black and yellow Fred Perry polo shirts along with red "Make America Great Again" hats.

A Proud Boy must declare that he is "a Western chauvinist who refuses to apologise for creating the modern world".

Their platform, such as it is, includes Trumpian ideas ("glorify the entrepreneur", "close the border"), libertarianism ("give everyone a gun", "end welfare") and traditional gender roles ("venerate the housewife").

They're not exclusively white and have become notorious for violent political confrontations.

The Proud Boys and affiliated groups have faced off against antifa in a number of violent street rallies in the last two years, most notably in Oregon, Washington and New York. Two members were jailed last year for beating up antifa activists in New York.

Facebook, Instagram, Twitter and YouTube have all banned the group from their platforms, and members and official chapters have been largely shunted towards less-popular networks.

Enrique Tarrio, the group's current chairman, reacted to the debate on the alternative discussion network Parler: "Standing by sir.... I will stand down sir!!!"

McInnes publicly disassociated himself from the group in 2018, saying that he was taking the advice of his legal team.

But in a video reacting to Tuesday's debate, he said (albeit not seeming entirely serious): "I control the Proud Boys, Donald. Do not stand down, do not stand back."

On the chat app Telegram, Proud Boys shared the debate clip along with posts taunting antifa and incorporating the phrase "stand back, stand by" into the group's logo.

Meanwhile, critics of the president loudly condemned him.

Antifa

Antifa, short for "anti-fascist", is a loose affiliation of mostly far-left activists.

They include anarchists, but also communists and a few social democrats. What sets them apart is their willingness to use violence—in self-defence, they say.

The movement, which at one point almost entirely disappeared in the US, saw a surge of interest after the election of Donald Trump. They routinely clash with the far right.

The group has been prominent during Black Lives Matter protests in many major cities, and have been particularly associated with unrest in Portland, Oregon.

In late August, a self-described anti-fascist, 48-year-old Michael Reinoehl, shot and killed a supporter of Patriot Prayer, a Portland-area group that often marches with the Proud Boys.

Reinoehl was shot dead by police the following week.

Both groups are relatively small—and can count on, at the most, a few thousand active supporters. But their propensity for violence, particularly when they confront each other on American streets, has made them a much bigger topic of conversation than those numbers suggest.

"Proud Boys and antifa—who are they and what do they want?" by Mike Wendling, BBC, September 30, 2020.

fearful, the more the strongmen can appear and say, 'I alone can fix it.'"

And "I alone can fix it" is a sentiment Americans have heard before—Trump said exactly that when he first accepted the Republican nomination in 2016.

Viewpoint 3

> *"By 1972, [George] Wallace's image was fixed in most Americans' minds as the face of the white South's violent response to the Civil Rights Movement. Wallace had skillfully deployed divisive, racially tinged attacks against liberals, government and protesters to become a serious contender for the presidency."*

Some Politicians Do Change Their Speech

Donald Nieman

In the following viewpoint, Donald Nieman argues that Governor George Wallace, a known racist and segregationist, changed his long-held beliefs and habits after surviving an assassination attempt. Nieman documents the changes that Wallace displayed after getting shot. Donald Nieman is a professor of history at Binghamton State University in New York and an authority on modern US law and politics. His writing has appeared in many outlets, including the Washington Post *and* Newsweek. *Nieman also has written several books on his area of specialty.*

As you read, consider the following questions:

1. What speech habits did Wallace employ to become a presidential candidate, as stated by Nieman?

2. What actions did Wallace take to try to make amends for his past behavior, according to Nieman?
3. Why do you think a brush with death changed Wallace's views?

Donald Trump's narrow escape from an assassin's bullet led me—a historian who has written about political polarization and the Civil Rights Movement—to think back to another norm-smashing populist who encountered death on the campaign trail: former Alabama governor and U.S. presidential candidate George Wallace.

By 1972, Wallace's image was fixed in most Americans' minds as the face of the white South's violent response to the Civil Rights Movement. Wallace had skillfully deployed divisive, racially tinged attacks against liberals, government and protesters to become a serious contender for the presidency.

So, Wallace turned heads when he publicly apologized and pleaded for forgiveness for his segregationist past after a 1972 assassination attempt at a campaign rally in Maryland left him paralyzed.

Facing death and seeking redemption

It's impossible to look into Wallace's heart and understand what moved him. Yet three factors probably loomed large.

First, the brush with death. It upended Wallace's life and forced him to end his 1972 bid for the presidency. It also left a pugnacious man who had been a boxer in his youth and was proud of his physical prowess bound to a wheelchair. He underwent frequent surgeries and lived in constant pain.

It's common for those who have faced death to reflect on their mortality and their life. Wallace was no exception.

Religion also may have played a role. While he was an earthy, profane man who didn't resist temptations of the flesh, Wallace couldn't escape the religious views that he had imbibed as a child and that permeated Southern culture. Faced with his own mortality, he thought about the fate of his soul and sought redemption by accepting Jesus, repenting and seeking forgiveness.

Less than a month after Wallace was shot, civil rights icon Shirley Chisholm visited him in his Maryland hospital room.

"I wouldn't want what happened to you to happen to anyone," she told the governor.

Wallace's daughter Peggy recalled that Chisholm's words brought her father to tears and he "started to change."

In 1974, Wallace professed his conversion in a speech at Jerry Falwell's Lynchburg, Virginia, megachurch. He told the congregation he had "been through the valley of the shadow of death," and proclaimed, "I am whole through the grace of our Lord and Savior, Jesus Christ."

Wallace reached out to those he had wronged, including John Lewis, the civil rights leader whose skull had been broken by Wallace's state troopers in Selma in 1965. Lewis was moved by their 1979 encounter.

"During that meeting, I could tell that he was a changed man; he was engaged in a campaign to seek forgiveness from the same African-Americans he had oppressed," Lewis wrote for *The New York Times* in 1998. "He acknowledged his bigotry and assumed responsibility for the harm he had caused. He wanted to be forgiven."

Playing to voters

Politics had been Wallace's life since he first won election to the Alabama Legislature in 1946. He could barely breathe without it, even after being nearly killed on the campaign trail.

"I don't believe he needs a family," his second wife, Cornelia, commented in the midst of an acrimonious divorce in 1978. "He just needs an audience."

Wallace's segregationist persona was a product, apparently, of politics. As a college student and budding politician, he was progressive by Southern standards: He avoided race-baiting and called for greater support for public services that benefited working-class Alabamians.

Years later, Ruth Johnson, whose husband, Frank, became a champion of civil rights as a federal judge, remembered Wallace as a college friend. "We were young and idealistic," Ruth recalled. "And we loved George for his enthusiasms."

In the late 1940s and 1950s, Wallace eschewed extremism. He refused to join the Dixiecrat rebellion against the Democratic Party's civil rights platform at the 1948 Democratic convention. And he had a reputation for dealing fairly with Black attorneys and plaintiffs during his years as a state judge.

That changed after he lost the Democratic nomination for governor in 1958 to a rival who courted the Ku Klux Klan and openly appealed to white racism. With the South in flames as the Civil Rights Movement accelerated, Wallace won election in 1962 as a full-throated segregationist.

"Segregation now, segregation tomorrow, segregation forever," he proclaimed in his 1963 inaugural address. Wallace physically confronted a U.S. deputy attorney general and federal marshals as they attempted to enforce a court order admitting a Black woman to the University of Alabama.

Going national

Ambitious and sensing that racism wasn't limited to the South, Wallace entered three Democratic presidential primaries in 1964 during his first term as governor. Then, after leaving office in 1967, he launched an unsuccessful third-party bid for the presidency in 1968.

He was reelected governor in 1970 and then pursued the Democratic presidential nomination in 1972 until his near-assassination. Despite his injuries, he remained in office, winning election to a third term and serving until 1979.

In 1983, even as Wallace's physical and mental condition deteriorated, he won a fourth term as governor. Being in the limelight was "a matter of life and death" for him, a long-term adviser observed.

The South had changed as a result of the movement Wallace fought so viciously, and Black people had become a major force in the Democratic Party. Ever the politician, Wallace changed too, appointing Black politicians to positions at all levels of his administration.

Wallace wasn't a saint. Two marriages ended in divorce, in part because of his emotional abuse of his wives.

Spike Lee's documentary "4 Little Girls," which recounts white supremacists' 1963 bombing of the 16th Street Baptist Church in Birmingham, Alabama, that killed four Black children, features chilling interviews with Wallace. They reveal a man who treated Black people who worked for him in the 1980s in an embarrassingly patronizing manner.

Still, Wallace reflected, repented and asked forgiveness. That's worth remembering at a time when many of us hope our leaders will become introspective and perhaps even change.

Viewpoint 4

> "...broader cultural, economic and political forces and attitudes have contributed to a resurgence in antisemitism—and other, similarly repellent forms of racial hatred in contemporary society."

Groups and Individuals Choose Hate Speech

Alexander Howard

In the following viewpoint, Alexander Howard outlines how political groups and celebrities have professed anti-democratic and racist viewpoints. Howard provides several examples of this behavior by examining statements by Gavin McInnes, founder of the Proud Boys, and celebrity Kanye West. Alexander Howard is a lecturer in the department of English and writing at the University of Sydney.

As you read, consider the following questions:

1. The founder of the Proud Boys dislikes which groups of people, as reported by Howard?
2. Which historical figure that most people find abhorrent does Kanye West appear to admire, according to this viewpoint?

3. How do Gavin McInnes and Kanye West differ, according to the author?

Gavin McInnes, founder of far-right "Western chauvinist" group the Proud Boys, told a BBC documentary that "the corrupt leftwing media" was responsible for the January 6 riot at the US Capitol, it emerged this week. The documentary also showed him saying he wants to "make America hate again".

"The left are the violent ones", McInnes told documentary makers. "We had one riot on January 6." Last year, Henry "Enrique" Tarrio, the Proud Boys' former national chairman, was sentenced to 22 years in prison for his part in the Capitol attack. Attorney-General Merrick Garland said the group "played a central role".

Jewish Australian journalist and documentary-maker John Safran met with McInnes in New York while researching his new book, *Squat*, which uses Kanye West's antisemitism as an entry to a range of topics.

In October 2022, West posted an antisemitic message on X, the social media platform previously known as Twitter:

> *I'm a bit sleepy tonight but when I wake up I'm going death con 3 on JEWISH PEOPLE.*

McInnes "was not a fan of transgender people, feminists or Muslims," Safran writes, "but he said he loved Jews. So much so that he met up with Kanye and tried to talk him out of promoting Hitler."

The central premise of this at times barely believable (but, as Safran maintains, absolutely true) book is Safran—who has a history of performing outlandish, occasionally shocking stunts—breaking into one of West's houses and squatting there for a week.

Safran employs his trademark mix of irreverence and sharp social commentary to create an entertaining—if sometimes frustratingly digressive—exploration of identity, religious hatred, conspiratorial thinking, and the toxicity of fame and celebrity culture.

Breaking Kanye's bubble

Dead of night. Rain pelting down. A solitary, slightly bedraggled figure laden with camping gear emerges from the thicket. He takes stock of his surroundings and sets off:

> *I don't need to scale a fence or wall to gain access. Instead, I need to jump down onto the brick patio. The drop is about my height if my head was sawn off.*

Safran is describing the moment he broke into Kanye West's house.

Sneaking inside, our intrepid trespasser discovers most of the interiors are painted the same shade of blue. He spends a week squatting there illegally, sleeping in the rapper's bed, rummaging through his cupboards and eating his pasta.

The house was actually a mansion—one of many properties owned by the eccentric recording artist now legally known as Ye. Located in Calabasas, one of the richest neighbourhoods in Los Angeles, it was totally abandoned. Weirdly, it was also wrapped in white plastic.

A disgruntled neighbour told Safran he thought the award-winning artist and trailblazing record producer wanted to fashion himself an enormous protective bubble.

Safran is unnerved by the scene. The rain striking the plastic sheets, the deserted rooms, the biblical scripture scrawled on the walls, and the vast, empty property all contribute to a feeling that something—or someone—might still be lurking nearby. But he rallies and decides to approach the eerie setting as an unexpected opportunity—a strange kind of writer's residency.

He builds a makeshift workstation, sits down and starts to write.

'A swastika on a sneaker'

Safran spent his adolescence listening to hip hop. As he wryly acknowledges, he "was possibly more into Public Enemy than the members of Public Enemy". However, by the time West released his debut album, *The College Dropout*, in 2004, Safran's musical palate had broadened.

He didn't pay much attention to West, who has a track record when it comes to provocative and offensive behaviour, until he started making antisemitic statements in public.

West's behaviour did not go down well with his business associates. In October 2022, the same month he made his inflammatory X statement, fashion house Balenciaga severed its ties with West, and Adidas ended the lucrative partnership that had played a pivotal role in elevating him to billionaire status.

As Safran recounts, it later emerged that during his decade-long collaboration with the German sporting giant, West "had allegedly drawn a swastika on a sneaker in a meeting with them and told a Jewish executive to kiss a picture of Adolf Hitler".

Now, Safran writes, West

> *wanted to get things off his chest publicly. He pushed the notion that Jews were cunning with money and greedier than non-Jews, tropes going back thousands of years.*

Things came to a head in December 2022, when West was interviewed on Infowars, the conspiracy theory platform hosted by Alex Jones. Wearing a black, eyeless balaclava with a bible on the desk, West began, as Safran says, "philosophising to millions".

Over the course of three hours, West made a series of disturbing remarks about the Nazis and the Holocaust. Even Jones—himself no stranger to performative outrage and antisemitic rhetoric—seemed genuinely taken aback.

In West's estimation, the "Germans had a really cool leader one time". That leader, he clarifies, was Adolf Hitler. He went on to assert that Jewish media outlets have "made us feel like the Nazis and Hitler have never offered anything of value to the world". West was unequivocal on this point. "Every human being has brought something of value. Especially Hitler."

Curious about Kanye's Nazi flirtation

Safran's grandparents left Poland, fleeing the Nazis, and settled in Melbourne soon after his mother was born in Uzbekistan. His previous books have covered racial violence (*Murder in Mississippi*, 2013) and political extremism (*Depends What You Mean by Extremist*, 2017).

So it's not surprising that West's statements piqued Safran's curiosity. He is also worried about the possible implications:

> *I mean, I dig his tunes, I like his lols and trolls, but he is still painting the Jews as maniacal. Some of his fans are going to take that and run with it.*

This explains why he booked a flight to Los Angeles. Safran's vague idea was to somehow track West down and, in his own words, "suss out what was going on". Specifically, he hoped to confront West and "start a conversation" about his antisemitism and admiration for genocidal maniacs.

Safran admits to being curious about West's true intentions:

> *Was Kanye's flirtation with Nazism actually Nazism? Or was it more a creative impulse, like painting Hitler on your nails because you thought it would be funny?*

Ultimately, those questions go unanswered. Try as he might, Safran never actually manages to bag a meeting with West. But he does get the chance to talk to several members of his extended entourage, each offering their own insights and perspectives on the controversial artist.

Celebrity culture and extremist ideologies

McInnes tells Safran racism no longer exists in the United States—even though he lives in a country where a presidential candidate accuses Haitian immigrants of eating pets and a comedian jokes at that candidate's event about Puerto Rico being a "floating island of garbage". McInnes also tells him he "agrees with Kanye that Jews controlled the levers of power, but, unlike Kanye, he thought that was a good thing".

Safran is perplexed. Encounters like this—and there are several—let him reflect on West's potential motives and patterns of behaviour. They also invite him to consider how broader cultural, economic and political forces and attitudes have contributed to a resurgence in antisemitism—and other, similarly repellent forms of racial hatred in contemporary society.

Through his interactions, Safran begins to piece together the ways these forces intersect with celebrity culture and extremist ideologies, offering an glimpse into how such noxious views have gained renewed traction in our digitally mediated dumpster fire of a world.

Significantly, *Squat* opens on the steps of the Sydney Opera House on October 8 2023, the scene of a contentious pro-Palestine rally. It offers insightful observations about antisemitism and conspiratorial extremism, which are much needed at this precise historical and geopolitical moment.

Yet Safran's style and tone—by turns circuitous and irreverent—at times jar and detract from the substance of the book. This is a pity, given the need for a serious, focused discussion of such matters at this historical and political juncture.

Viewpoint 5

> *"The war has raised humanitarian concerns beyond northern Gaza."*

Global Events May Explain Increase in Hate Speech

The Center for Preventative Action

In the following viewpoint, the Center for Preventative Action outlines the Israeli-Palestinian conflict from its beginnings to the current situation, as of this writing, in 2025. The Center for Preventative Action provides a balanced analysis of this historic conflict between Israel and the Palestinians. The Center for Preventative Action presents information for the Council on Foreign Relations.

As you read, consider the following questions:

1. Why is the Israeli-Palestinian conflict politically contentious?
2. How have past events contributed to the current war?
3. Which other countries have involved themselves or been drawn into the conflict?

Hamas launched its deadly attack on Israel on October 7, 2023, prompting the Israel Defense Forces (IDF) to engage in aerial campaigns and ground operations within the Gaza Strip. On

"Israeli-Palestinian Conflict" by By the Center for Preventive Action, Council on Foreign Relations, October 06, 2024.From CFR.org. Reprinted with permission. For more analysis and social issues and foreign policy, visit CFR.org.

January 15, 2025, the United States, Egypt, and Qatar announced that they had mediated a cease-fire between Israel and Hamas to end fifteen months of fighting in Gaza. Hamas released thirty-three of the remaining hostages, while Israel released hundreds of Palestinians from Israeli jails, displaced residents were allowed to return to northern Gaza, and 600 humanitarian aid trucks were permitted to enter the territory each day. However, Israel launched a wave of strikes and ground operations in central and southern Gaza on March 18, bringing an end to the six-week cease-fire.

The conflict has exacerbated regional tensions across the Middle East. The IDF launched a ground invasion of Lebanon following months of cross-border skirmishes with Hezbollah, which began striking northern Israel following Hamas's October 7 attack. Yemen's Houthi rebels have shot missiles at Israel and commercial ships in the Red Sea, and other Iran-backed groups have launched dozens of attacks on U.S. military positions in Iraq and Syria. In April and October of 2024, Iran took the unprecedented step of attacking Israel directly, which prompted Israeli counterstrikes targeting Iranian air defenses and missile manufacturing facilities.

Background

The Israeli-Palestinian conflict dates back to the end of the nineteenth century. In 1947, the United Nations adopted Resolution 181, known as the Partition Plan, which sought to divide the British Mandate of Palestine into Arab and Jewish states. On May 14, 1948, the State of Israel was created, sparking the first Arab-Israeli War. The war ended in 1949 with Israel's victory, but 750,000 Palestinians were displaced, and the territory was divided into 3 parts: the State of Israel, the West Bank (of the Jordan River), and the Gaza Strip.

Over the following years, tensions rose in the region, particularly between Israel and Egypt, Jordan, and Syria. Following the 1956 Suez Crisis and Israel's invasion of the Sinai Peninsula, Egypt, Jordan, and Syria signed mutual defense pacts in anticipation of a possible mobilization of Israeli troops. In June 1967, following a series of maneuvers by Egyptian President

Abdel Gamal Nasser, Israel preemptively attacked Egyptian and Syrian air forces, starting the Six-Day War. After the war, Israel gained territorial control over the Sinai Peninsula and Gaza Strip from Egypt; the West Bank and East Jerusalem from Jordan; and the Golan Heights from Syria.

Six years later, in what is referred to as the Yom Kippur War or the October War, Egypt and Syria launched a surprise two-front attack on Israel to regain their lost territory; the conflict did not result in significant gains for Egypt, Israel, or Syria, but Egyptian President Anwar al-Sadat declared the war a victory for Egypt as it allowed Egypt and Syria to negotiate over previously ceded territory. Finally, in 1979, following a series of cease-fires and peace negotiations, representatives from Egypt and Israel signed the Camp David Accords, a peace treaty that ended the thirty-year conflict between Egypt and Israel.

Even though the Camp David Accords improved relations between Israel and its neighbors, the question of Palestinian self-determination and self-governance remained unresolved. In 1987, hundreds of thousands of Palestinians living in the West Bank and Gaza Strip rose up against the Israeli government in what is known as the first intifada. The 1993 Oslo I Accords mediated the conflict, setting up a framework for the Palestinians to govern themselves in the West Bank and Gaza, and enabled mutual recognition between the newly established Palestinian Authority and Israel's government. In 1995, the Oslo II Accords expanded on the first agreement, adding provisions that mandated the complete withdrawal of Israel from 6 cities and 450 towns in the West Bank.

In 2000, sparked in part by Palestinian grievances over Israel's control over the West Bank, a stagnating peace process, and former Israeli Prime Minister Ariel Sharon's visit to the al-Aqsa mosque—the third holiest site in Islam—in September 2000, Palestinians launched the second intifada, which would last until 2005. In response, the Israeli government approved the construction of a barrier wall around the West Bank in 2002, despite opposition from the International Court of Justice and the International Criminal Court.

Factionalism among the Palestinians flared up when Hamas won the Palestinian Authority's parliamentary elections in 2006, deposing longtime majority party Fatah. This gave Hamas, a political and militant movement inspired by the Palestinian Muslim Brotherhood, control of the Gaza Strip. Gaza is a small piece of land on the Mediterranean Sea that borders Egypt to the south and has been under the rule of the semi-autonomous Palestinian Authority since 1993. The United States and European Union, among others, did not acknowledge Hamas' electoral victory, as the group has been considered a terrorist organization by western governments since the late 1990s. Following Hamas' seizure of control, violence broke out between Hamas and Fatah. Between 2006 and 2011, a series of failed peace talks and deadly confrontations culminated in an agreement to reconcile. Fatah entered into a unity government with Hamas in 2014.

In the summer of 2014, clashes in the Palestinian territories precipitated a military confrontation between the Israeli military and Hamas in which Hamas fired nearly three thousand rockets at Israel, and Israel retaliated with a major offensive in Gaza. The skirmish ended in late August 2014 with a cease-fire deal brokered by Egypt, but only after 73 Israelis and 2,251 Palestinians were killed. After a wave of violence between Israelis and Palestinians in 2015, Palestinian President Mahmoud Abbas of Fatah announced that Palestinians would no longer be bound by the territorial divisions created by the Oslo Accords.

In March of 2018, Israeli troops killed 183 Palestinians and wounded 6,000 others after some Palestinians stormed the perimeter fence between the Gaza Strip and Israel and threw rocks during an otherwise peaceful demonstration. Just months later, Hamas militants fired over one hundred rockets into Israel, and Israel responded with strikes on more than fifty targets in Gaza during a twenty-four-hour flare-up. The tense political atmosphere resulted in a return to disunity between Fatah and

Hamas, with Mahmoud Abbas' Fatah party controlling the Palestinian Authority from the West Bank and Hamas de facto ruling the Gaza Strip.

The Donald J. Trump administration reversed longstanding U.S. policy by canceling funding for the UN Relief and Works Agency, which provides aid to Palestinian refugees, and relocating the U.S. embassy from Tel Aviv to Jerusalem. The Trump administration also helped broker the Abraham Accords, under which Bahrain and the United Arab Emirates normalized relations with Israel, becoming only the third and fourth countries in the region—following Egypt in 1979 and Jordan in 1994—to do so. Similar deals followed with Morocco and Sudan. Palestinian leader Mahmoud Abbas of Fatah rejected the accords, as did Hamas.

In early May 2021, after a court ruled in favor of the eviction of several Palestinian families from East Jerusalem properties, protests erupted, with Israeli police employing force against demonstrators. After several consecutive days of violence, Hamas, the militant group that governs Gaza, and other Palestinian militant groups launched hundreds of rockets into Israeli territory. Israel responded with artillery bombardments and airstrikes, killing more than twenty Palestinians and hitting both military and non-military infrastructure, including residential buildings, media headquarters, and refugee and healthcare facilities. After eleven days, Israel and Hamas agreed to a cease-fire, with both sides claiming victory. The fighting killed more than 250 Palestinians and at least 13 Israelis, wounded nearly 2,000 others, and displaced 72,000 Palestinians.

The most far-right and religious government in Israel's history, led by Benjamin 'Bibi' Netanyahu and his Likud party and comprising two ultra-Orthodox parties and three far-right parties, was inaugurated in late December 2022. The coalition government prioritized the expansion and development of Israeli settlements in the occupied West Bank, endorsed discrimination against LGBTQ+ people on religious grounds, and voted to limit judicial oversight of the government in May 2023 after a delay due to nationwide protests in March.

Recent Developments

In early October 2023, Hamas fighters fired rockets into Israel and stormed southern Israeli cities and towns across the border of the Gaza Strip in a surprise attack, killing more than 1,300 Israelis, injuring 3,300, and taking hundreds of hostages. One day after the October 7 attack, the Israeli cabinet formally declared war against Hamas, followed by a directive from the defense minister to the Israel Defense Forces (IDF) to carry out a "complete siege" of Gaza. It is the most significant escalation of the Israeli-Palestinian conflict in several decades.

Israel ordered over one million Palestinian civilians in northern Gaza to evacuate ahead of a ground invasion that commenced on October 27 in conjunction with Israel's continued aerial assault. From November 24 to November 30, 2023, a temporary truce facilitated the exchange of certain Israeli hostages for Palestinian prisoners held in Israeli jails, as well as a surge in humanitarian aid to the Strip. However, hostilities resumed following reports of violations by both Israeli and Hamas forces.

In January 2024, under pressure from its principal ally, the United States, and amid global scrutiny both over the humanitarian crisis in Gaza and doubts about the feasibility of completely eradicating Hamas, Israel signaled its intent to shift to lower-intensity operations in Gaza. The IDF also started to shift its focus from northern Gaza to prepare for a campaign in southern Gaza, including in the city of Rafah.

Israel's push for a Rafah operation prompted a public backlash from the Biden administration. In May 2024, news outlets broke that the United States had paused a shipment of bombs to Israel. Administration officials cited concerns that the weapons—primarily 2,000-pound bombs—could cause an unacceptable number of civilian casualties if used in Rafah's dense, urban environment, where over a million Gazan civilians were sheltering at the time.

A week later, President Biden publicly stated that he had warned Netanyahu the United States would withhold certain offensive weapons, including bombs and artillery shells, if the Israeli military launched an operation Rafah. The Biden administration ultimately did not act on this threat as it determined Israel's campaign in Rafah was sufficiently more targeted than its earlier operations during the war.

In the fall of 2024, while continuing operations in southern and central Gaza, the IDF launched a renewed offensive in northern Gaza, specifically around the Jabalia refugee camp. The stated goal was to eliminate Hamas militants who had begun regrouping in the area and filling the vacuum left after the Israeli military's earlier operations. The IDF's operations in Jabalia raised concerns among experts that Israel might be planning to implement the controversial "Generals' Plan," which advocates for a total siege of the area, including the withholding of humanitarian aid, to force the surrender of remaining Hamas militants. Between October 6 and December 31, 2024, the UN attempted to reach the besieged area 165 times. Of those attempts, Israeli authorities denied 149, while the remaining 16 faced impediments.

The war has raised humanitarian concerns beyond northern Gaza. Since the start of Israeli operations in 2023, multiple reports have documented the targeting of journalists, schools, and Israeli-designated humanitarian zones. Repeated Israeli attacks on medical sites, including hospitals and critical infrastructure, have led to a surge in diseases such as polio throughout the Strip. Violence against humanitarian workers has further exacerbated the crisis. In April 2024, an Israeli airstrike killed seven employees of the World Central Kitchen, and World Food Programme workers were shot in August of that year. These incidents have created a chilling effect on humanitarian agencies operating in Gaza, with many suspending or limiting their operations until they can better ensure their employees' safety. Additionally, Israel's ban on many dual-use items in Gaza has hindered humanitarian aid operations. In its efforts to prevent items with potential military applications from reaching Hamas, Israeli inspectors have rejected critical supplies, such as chlorine tablets for water purification, brought in by humanitarian organizations.

As of January 2025, 1.9 million Gazans—about 90 percent of Gaza's population—have been displaced and are categorized as facing acute or catastrophic food insecurity. There are currently no functioning hospitals in Gaza. The war has led to over 46,000 Gazan deaths, of which the Israeli military estimates 17,000 were Hamas militants. Israel has argued in many cases that its actions were necessary because Hamas's guerilla warfare tactics often involve fighters embedding themselves in civilian areas. The military has also cited military successes, including the June 2024 rescue of four living hostages in central Gaza and the elimination of Hamas's top leadership, including the group's leader Yahya Sinwar, military chief Mohammed Deif, and Deif's deputy Marwan Issa. However, the United States has cautioned that it assesses Hamas has been able to recruit replacements for nearly all the fighters that it has lost so far due to the war's radicalizing effects on Gazans.

Viewpoint 6

> *"Israel has fundamental legal obligations to abide by during its campaign against Hamas."*

International Law and the Israel-Hamas War

David J. Scheffer

In the following viewpoint, David J. Scheffer analyzes the Israel-Hamas war through the lens of international humanitarian law. David J. Scheffer is a senior fellow at the Council on Foreign Relations focusing on international law and international criminal justice.

As you read, consider the following questions:

1. What does international humanitarian law protect during war, as reported by the viewpoint?
2. According to the viewpoint, what geographic areas define the state of Palestine?
3. What effect does international humanitarian law have on both Israel and Hamas, as stated by Scheffer?

The atrocities Hamas committed against Israel on October 7 have sent shockwaves around the world and prompted the Israeli government to embark on a war of still-unknown magnitude and character against the Palestinian militant group.

Israel's military campaign in the Gaza Strip seeks to fulfill several objectives, including the destruction of Hamas and the rescue of hostages, that are strictly regulated by international law. Observing these legal guardrails, as Israel has declared it will do, will make the conflict complicated and risky, particularly because Israel's actions will be scrutinized by various observers, including other governments, the United Nations, the International Criminal Court, legal scholars, civil society, and the general public. The large number of civilian casualties in a fiery explosion at a Gaza hospital has underscored how an unconstrained war could take a grim human toll.

Hamas's war crimes

Hamas's killing of at least 1400 Israeli civilians (including children) during its surprise attack on Israeli territory violated provisions of international humanitarian law that are designed to protect civilians and their property during war. They include Common Article 3 of the 1949 Geneva Conventions, which requires humane treatment of civilians and noncombatants; Article 51 of the conventions' Protocol I, which protects civilian populations from attack; and a host of provisions on war crimes and crimes against humanity in Articles 7 and 8 of the Rome Statute of the International Criminal Court (ICC), which reflect customary international law and apply to Hamas leaders and fighters. Moreover, Hamas's continuous, indiscriminate rocket attacks against Israeli targets put civilian structures and individuals at risk, also violating these treaty provisions and customary international law.

Is Hamas covered by international law?

There continues to be a rather strained debate among governments and legal scholars about applying various fields of international law to nonstate actors such as Hamas, including questions about the legal obligations of states that these actors come into conflict with. For example, in the United States, the George W. Bush administration advanced a "legal black hole" argument during the so-called war on terrorism that followed 9/11, claiming that al-Qaeda and the Taliban were nonstate actors and therefore unprotected by the 1949 Geneva Conventions. However, the U.S. Supreme Court discredited that legal argument in 2006, ruling that Common Article 3 of the conventions did apply to the U.S. war with al-Qaeda.

Israel and the "state of Palestine," which is recognized by most countries as comprising the West Bank, Gaza, and East Jerusalem, are ratified parties of the four Geneva Conventions of 1949. Israel has not ratified the first and second protocols of the conventions, which in 1977 further regulated protection of civilians, property, and the environment during war. One of the prominent provisions is Article 75 of Protocol I, which Washington has long viewed as part of customary international law and thus the provision would bind not only the United States but also Israel. It requires that persons held by a combatant power shall be treated humanely in all circumstances and provides a detailed list of prohibited conduct. A plurality of Supreme Court justices in the 2006 decision stressed Article 75's customary application. Palestine has ratified all three protocols, so as a state party, it is undeniably bound to their terms. Hamas, particularly as a de facto governing authority in Palestine (namely, over Gaza) with control over its own militant forces, is obligated as part of the state of Palestine to comply with the Geneva Conventions and its three protocols.

The state of Palestine also is a state party of the Rome Statute of the International Criminal Court (ICC), which means that Hamas leaders and personnel can be held accountable for committing genocide, crimes against humanity, or war crimes on, for example, Israeli territory or in Gaza. Israel, like the United States and dozens of other countries, is not a state party of the Rome Statute, but the ICC prosecutor will scrutinize its military actions in Gaza, the territory of a state party.

Israel's self-defense

Israel's primary objectives are self-defense in response to the Hamas attacks and ensuring the future security of Israel. Article 51 of the

UN Charter permits actions of "inherent" self-defense derived from customary international law, and it does not limit that right to actions against the conventional armed forces of another state. The UN Security Council can choose not to take any action to reinforce or circumscribe this right of self-defense—and, regardless, the body has long been essentially paralyzed by the fracture between Western permanent members and the twosome of Russia and China, as amply demonstrated during the council's inconclusive meeting on October 16.

Deeply associated with Israel's self-defense measures is the government's stated intention to terminate Hamas entirely. International law does not explicitly prohibit the use of force to eliminate an organization such as Hamas, which Israel, the United States, and many other countries consider a terrorist group. It remains important, however, that Israel's use of force to achieve this aim abides by the right of self-defense under the UN Charter and is in accordance with the law of armed conflict and international humanitarian law.

What should Israel do to comply with international humanitarian law?

Israel has fundamental legal obligations to abide by during its campaign against Hamas. Heavily charged statements by some Israeli officials need to be separated from sound legal policy. In brief, Israel must meet several standards:

- It must not use starvation (including deprivation of food, water, and other essentials for survival) of Gaza's civilian population as a weapon of war against Hamas or for any reason.
- It must take every possible step to target only Hamas militants and their military infrastructure, and to minimize civilian casualties and the destruction of civilian infrastructure. The Israeli air and artillery campaign, as well as its ground warfare, must be guided by the immutable legal principles of humanity, distinction, proportionality, and military necessity.

- It must allow for the return of displaced civilians after the conflict. While a temporary evacuation of civilians from a theater of combat can be legally requested, it would be unlawful to permanently displace the civilian population from their homes. The circumstances in Gaza today create enormous hardship for hundreds of thousands of Palestinian civilians, and Israel should take measures to ameliorate these difficult conditions. The visits of U.S. President Joe Biden and U.S. Secretary of State Antony Blinken to the Middle East this week focused in part on what Israel and other nations and organizations can do to address the humanitarian plight of Palestinians in Gaza.

Rescuing hostages

Another paramount objective for Israel is the rescue or release of the roughly two-hundred Israeli, American, and other foreign hostages. Hamas's taking of hostages from Israeli territory and using them, illegally, as human shields in Gaza under life-imperiling conditions pose particular challenges for Israeli military action. If Hamas had not taken hostages, Israel's strategy for confronting the militant group might have been different.

Though much debated among international lawyers and governments, there is a legal right for states to use force to rescue hostages, as long as their actions meet four criteria:

- many hostages are seized, particularly during an armed attack (as occurred on October 7),
- the actions are necessary (there is a threat of violence against Hamas's hostages, and non-forcible recovery options, such as a negotiated deal with the group, may prove futile),
- there is an immediacy (a quickly negotiated release is not possible, and the fate of the hostages appears to worsen with each passing day), and
- the use of force is proportional (using only the level of armed force that is necessary to rescue the hostages).

The final criterion of proportionality would be superseded by the anticipated Israeli incursion into Gaza because that intervention would be made under the right of self-defense—a much larger-scale objective—and not only to rescue the hostages.

Whatever the debate may be about Palestinian statehood, the applicability of various treaties, and whether Israel is an occupying power over Gaza, Israel should take care to follow the powerful requirements of customary international law as it defends itself against Hamas and pursues the rescue of hostages.

Periodical and Internet Sources Bibliography

The following articles have been selected to supplement the diverse views presented in this chapter.

Daniel L. Byman, "How Hateful Rhetoric Connects to Real-World Violence," Brookings, April 9, 2021. www.brookings.edu/articles/how-hateful-rhetoric-connects-to-real-world-violence/.

Erica Chenowith, "Threat, Emboldenment, or Both? The Effects of Political Power on Violent Hate Crimes," Harvard Kennedy School, November 2020. www.hks.harvard.edu/publications/threat-emboldenment-or-both-effects-political-power-violent-hate-crimes.

Sofia Cherici, "Mirroring Bias: Online Hate Speech and Polarisation," *Green European Journal*, July 2, 2021. www.greeneuropeanjournal.eu/mirroring-bias-online-hate-speech-and-polarisation/.

Emily Ekins, "The State of Free Speech and Tolerance in America," Cato Institute, October 31, 2017. www.cato.org/survey-reports/state-free-speech-tolerance-america.

Mark Follman, "Trump Amplifies His Dangerous Hate Speech Against Migrants," *Mother Jones*, September 30, 2024. www.motherjones.com/politics/2024/09/trump-hate-speech-migrants-campaign-rallies-incitement/.

Max Hoffman, "Will Viktor Orban Bring His Racist Rhetoric to the United States This Week," CAP, August 3, 2022. www.americanprogress.org/article/will-viktor-orban-bring-his-racist-rhetoric-to-the-united-states-this-week/.

Jannika Jahn, "Strong on Hate Speech, Too Strict on Political Debate," Verfassungsblog, May 25, 2023. verfassungsblog.de/strong-on-hate-speech-too-strict-on-political-debate/.

Rachel Kleinfeld, "The Rise of Political Violence in the United States," *Journal of Democracy*, October 2021. www.journalofdemocracy.org/articles/the-rise-of-political-violence-in-the-united-states/.

Ronald Niezen, "Aliens and Animals- Language of Hate Used by Trump and Others Can Be Part of a Violent Design," *The Conversation*, January 29, 2025. theconversation.com/aliens-and-animals-language-of-hate-used-by-trump-and-others-can-be-part-of-a-violent-design-245524.

Sara Pequeno, "Trump's Hateful Speech Riled Up Republicans. It's Clear GOP Won't Stand Up to Him," *USA Today*, March 5, 2025. www.usatoday.com/story/opinion/columnist/2025/03/05/trump-speech-targets-trans-people-gender/81497808007/.

Justin Spike, "How Hungary's Orban Uses Control of the Media to Escape Scrutiny and Keep the Public in the Dark," AP, July 31, 2024. www.ap.org/news-highlights/spotlights/2024/how-hungarys-orban-uses-control-of-the-media-to-escape-scrutiny-and-keep-the-public-in-the-dark/.

Myah Ward, "We Watched 20 Trump Rallies. His Racist, Anti-Immigrant Messaging is Getting Darker," Politico, October 12, 2024. https://www.politico.com/news/2024/10/12/trump-racist-rhetoric-immigrants-00183537.

OPPOSING VIEWPOINTS® SERIES

Chapter 3

Does Cultural Identity Play a Role in Hate Speech and Hate Groups?

Chapter Preface

Throughout history, humans have separated themselves into various groups, based on things such as skin color, sexual orientation, religious affiliation, and much more. Many people base their identity on the groups they belong to. While people from different cultures can and do get along, some people feel that their own sense of identity is threatened by people whose cultural identity is vastly different than their own.

Several viewpoint articles in this chapter explore what role culture and cultural identity play in hate speech and hate groups. An obvious question is whether social media, which has an oversized grasp on modern culture, has any influence on people's behavior. Many people have questioned whether the influence of media is good, bad, or neutral. Does social media push unverified falsehoods? Is social media contributing to outlandish conspiracy theories? Do either of these cause people to feel hate toward others? With further thought, can social media be an aid to young people while causing them to see people different from themselves as objects of dislike?

One viewpoint author explores how the Nazi party in Germany took control over the country's youth and transformed them into a group which believed Nazi propaganda and hate. A sidebar analyzes another pre-social media hate group, the KKK. Still another viewpoint author outlines the growth of European right-wing groups that target immigrants. Finally, one viewpoint article spotlights resistance of hate speech and genocide.

Viewpoint 1

> *"As more and more people have moved online, experts say, individuals inclined toward racism, misogyny, or homophobia have found niches that can reinforce their views and goad them to violence. Social media platforms also offer violent actors the opportunity to publicize their acts."*

Does Social Media Contribute to Hate Speech and Hate Crimes?

Zachary Laub

In the following viewpoint, Zachary Laub analyzes the intersection between hate speech and social media. Laub maintains that violent acts are encouraged by individuals espousing hate speech on social media sites. Laub argues that this is happening around the world and provides examples to back his claims. Finally, Laub explains how social media companies attempt to police inappropriate content on their sites. Zachary Laub writes for the Council on Foreign Relations.

As you read, consider the following questions:

1. Is hate speech on social media an isolated occurrence, as reported by Laub?

2. Where around the globe have individuals espousing hate speech used social media to further their cause, according to the viewpoint?
3. According to the author, how do social media platforms enforce appropriate activity on their sites?

A mounting number of attacks on immigrants and other minorities has raised new concerns about the connection between inflammatory speech online and violent acts, as well as the role of corporations and the state in policing speech. Analysts say trends in hate crimes around the world echo changes in the political climate, and that social media can magnify discord. At their most extreme, rumors and invective disseminated online have contributed to violence ranging from lynchings to ethnic cleansing.

The response has been uneven, and the task of deciding what to censor, and how, has largely fallen to the handful of corporations that control the platforms on which much of the world now communicates. But these companies are constrained by domestic laws. In liberal democracies, these laws can serve to defuse discrimination and head off violence against minorities. But such laws can also be used to suppress minorities and dissidents.

How widespread is the problem?

Incidents have been reported on nearly every continent. Much of the world now communicates on social media, with nearly a third of the world's population active on Facebook alone. As more and more people have moved online, experts say, individuals inclined toward racism, misogyny, or homophobia have found niches that can reinforce their views and goad them to violence. Social media platforms also offer violent actors the opportunity to publicize their acts.

Social scientists and others have observed how social media posts, and other online speech, can inspire acts of violence:

- In Germany a correlation was found between anti-refugee Facebook posts by the far-right Alternative for Germany party and attacks on refugees. Scholars Karsten Muller and Carlo Schwarz observed that upticks in attacks, such as arson and assault, followed spikes in hate-mongering posts.
- In the United States, perpetrators of recent white supremacist attacks have circulated among racist communities online, and also embraced social media to publicize their acts. Prosecutors said the Charleston church shooter, who killed nine black clergy and worshippers in June 2015, engaged in a "self-learning process" online that led him to believe that the goal of white supremacy required violent action.
- The 2018 Pittsburgh synagogue shooter was a participant in the social media network Gab, whose lax rules have attracted extremists banned by larger platforms. There, he espoused the conspiracy that Jews sought to bring immigrants into the United States, and render whites a minority, before killing eleven worshippers at a refugee-themed Shabbat service. This "great replacement" trope, which was heard at the white supremacist rally in Charlottesville, Virginia, a year prior and originates with the French far right, expresses demographic anxieties about nonwhite immigration and birth rates.
- The great replacement trope was in turn espoused by the perpetrator of the 2019 New Zealand mosque shootings, who killed forty-nine Muslims at prayer and sought to broadcast the attack on YouTube.
- In Myanmar, military leaders and Buddhist nationalists used social media to slur and demonize the Rohingya Muslim minority ahead of and during a campaign of ethnic cleansing. Though Rohingya comprised perhaps 2 percent of the population, ethnonationalists claimed that Rohingya would soon supplant the Buddhist majority. The UN fact-finding mission said, "Facebook has been a useful instrument for

those seeking to spread hate, in a context where, for most users, Facebook is the Internet."

- In India, lynch mobs and other types of communal violence, in many cases originating with rumors on WhatsApp groups, have been on the rise since the Hindu-nationalist Bharatiya Janata Party (BJP) came to power in 2014.
- Sri Lanka has similarly seen vigilantism inspired by rumors spread online, targeting the Tamil Muslim minority. During a spate of violence in March 2018, the government blocked access to Facebook and WhatsApp, as well as the messaging app Viber, for a week, saying that Facebook had not been sufficiently responsive during the emergency.

Does social media catalyze hate crimes?

The same technology that allows social media to galvanize democracy activists can be used by hate groups seeking to organize and recruit. It also allows fringe sites, including peddlers of conspiracies, to reach audiences far broader than their core readership. Online platforms' business models depend on maximizing reading or viewing times. Since Facebook and similar platforms make their money by enabling advertisers to target audiences with extreme precision, it is in their interests to let people find the communities where they will spend the most time.

Users' experiences online are mediated by algorithms designed to maximize their engagement, which often inadvertently promote extreme content. Some web watchdog groups say YouTube's autoplay function, in which the player, at the end of one video, tees up a related one, can be especially pernicious. The algorithm drives people to videos that promote conspiracy theories or are otherwise "divisive, misleading or false," according to a *Wall Street Journal* investigative report. "YouTube may be one of the most powerful radicalizing instruments of the 21st century," writes sociologist Zeynep Tufekci.

YouTube said in June 2019 that changes to its recommendation algorithm made in January had halved views of videos deemed "borderline content" for spreading misinformation. At that time, the company also announced that it would remove neo-Nazi and white supremacist videos from its site. Yet the platform faced criticism that its efforts to curb hate speech do not go far enough. For instance, critics note that rather than removing videos that provoked homophobic harassment of a journalist, YouTube instead cut off the offending user from sharing in advertising revenue.

How do platforms enforce their rules?

Social media platforms rely on a combination of artificial intelligence, user reporting, and staff known as content moderators to enforce their rules regarding appropriate content. Moderators, however, are burdened by the sheer volume of content and the trauma that comes from sifting through disturbing posts, and social media companies don't evenly devote resources across the many markets they serve.

A ProPublica investigation found that Facebook's rules are opaque to users and inconsistently applied by its thousands of contractors charged with content moderation. (Facebook says there are fifteen thousand.) In many countries and disputed territories, such as the Palestinian territories, Kashmir, and Crimea, activists and journalists have found themselves censored, as Facebook has sought to maintain access to national markets or to insulate itself from legal liability. "The company's hate-speech rules tend to favor elites and governments over grassroots activists and racial minorities," ProPublica found.

Viewpoint 2

> *"The Nazis intended their ideology to live on for centuries, so young people were an essential part of their long-term plan. By plaguing the education system with Nazi propaganda and creating organizations like the Hitler Youth, they indoctrinated the younger generations, capturing their minds with powerful imagery and inspirational rhetoric."*

German Nazi Culture Brainwashed German Youth

Jacob Wilkins

In the following viewpoint, Jacob Wilkins outlines how the Nazi Party in Germany effectively brainwashed the youth of the country to its sinister actions. Wilkins outlines how children, parents, and teachers changed in Germany. Wilkins also explains what place book burning and propaganda played in the Nazi scheme. Interestingly, Wilkins notes that after the defeat of Hitler, not all Germans agreed with democratization. Jacob Wilkins is a freelance writer.

As you read, consider the following questions:

1. Why did parents want their sons to join the Hitler Youth, as stated by the viewpoint?
2. According to Wilkins, how was school different for German youth because of the Nazis?
3. What were three youth groups that resisted the Nazis, as stated by the author?

The Hitler Youth was a frightening and powerful organization, but it was just one of the many ways the Nazis captured the minds of Germany's youth.

Many consider the Nazis to be the most sinister political party of all time, and it's hard to argue with this point. Driven by a fervent belief in the superiority of the Aryan race, they transformed Germany into a fascist state and carried out one of the worst crimes in human history: the Holocaust.

The Nazis intended their ideology to live on for centuries, so young people were an essential part of their long-term plan. By plaguing the education system with Nazi propaganda and creating organizations like the Hitler Youth, they indoctrinated the younger generations, capturing their minds with powerful imagery and inspirational rhetoric.

Life in the Hitler Youth

Back in 1925, Hitler stressed the importance of physical exercise in *Mein Kampf*. He believed a strong body was the foundation of a strong mind and that physical development was a matter for the state, not the individual.

The Hitler Youth put these principles into practice. The organization aimed to turn boys into soldiers who would fight for the Nazis' cause. Boys in the Hitler Youth engaged in plenty of physical activity, working on their conditioning and developing their sense of camaraderie. Activities like hiking and camping complemented sports like boxing, swimming, and running.

Boys in the Hitler Youth also watched Nazi propaganda films. These films depicted young men competing in athletics events, learning to march, working outdoors, hiking up mountains, and using equipment like maps, compasses, rifles, and grenades.

Those who didn't join the Hitler Youth could be refused their school leaving certificate, barring them from getting an apprenticeship or a job. This pushed parents to ensure their child joined the Hitler Youth, and by 1939, membership was just under nine million.

Alongside the indoctrination of teenagers, there was another division of the Hitler Youth aimed at younger boys, who joined up when they were just ten years old.

Brainwashing the Girls of Germany

The female counterpart of the Hitler Youth was called the League of German Girls. This organization brainwashed girls into believing they should be healthy, fertile housewives who reared the next generation. Physical education was paramount once again, with a particular focus on athletics and gymnastics. This led to tension within the organization, as some felt the girls were becoming masculinized.

Alongside their exercise routines, the girls took part in domestic and agricultural activities, including the Women's Labour Service. This six-month working period in either the agricultural or domestic sector became mandatory in 1939. The girls also attended political rallies and meetings with members of the Hitler Youth and entertained crowds by singing at festivals in Germany.

Like the Hitler Youth, there was also a younger division that allowed girls to join up when they were ten years old.

Nazi Propaganda in the Classroom

Even those who managed to escape the clutches of the youth organizations couldn't evade Nazi propaganda indefinitely.

Schools became hubs of indoctrination, with children facing Nazi propaganda before they even opened a textbook. School buildings featured swastika signs and portraits of Hitler and Nazi flags in the playground.

Though certain subjects, like maths and physics, didn't alter too much, others underwent dramatic changes. In biology lessons, teachers emphasized racial purity, contrasting the superiority of the Aryan child (often depicted with stereotypically blonde hair and blue eyes) against members of the Jewish community. Teachers told girls to be selective with their marital partners, encouraging them to keep bloodlines pure and avoid interracial breeding.

Just like the Nazi youth organizations, schools placed great importance on physical health. In 1934, the Nazis brought back the three-lessons-a-week exercise schedule (previously removed under the Weimar Republic). In addition to making children healthier, physical education was also designed to teach leadership skills and provide the boys with the mentality of a soldier.

As for essay-based subjects, students were required to write essays on topics such as Hitler's place in history, the inferiority of Jews, or the writer Horst Wessel, a Nazi supporter who became a martyr after he was killed by communists. Geography lessons were plagued by Nazi propaganda as well, with textbooks emphasizing geopolitics, the expansion of Germanic tribes throughout history, and German superiority.

To ensure their principles would be upheld in the classroom, the Nazis purged public school systems of Jewish teachers and those who were politically opposed to the new regime. But most teachers went along with the changes without complaint. Indeed, teachers joined the Nazi Party in greater numbers than any other profession.

In 1937, the Nazis expanded their educational scheme even further by establishing Adolf Hitler Schools. These institutions were exclusive and selective. Potential students had to take an entrance exam that tested their judgment, comprehension, ingenuity, and retention. When the selection process was complete, the primary aim of these schools was to develop the leadership skills of their students.

Book Burnings & Higher Education

The Nazification of higher education was surprisingly easy, as plenty of young adults supported the Nazis before they came to power in 1933.

Spearheaded by Joseph Goebbels, the Nazi propaganda machine targeted Germany's youth by portraying themselves as a fresh, forward-looking party that could unshackle the country from the chains of the Weimar Republic. Alongside traditional propaganda methods like posters and pamphlets, the Nazis channeled their message through the modern media, using tools like films and radio broadcasts to appeal to the youth of Germany.

The Nazis emphasized their love of the homeland and the preservation of the nation. These patriotic values stood out against the rhetoric of Germany's moderate politicians, who often focused on the country's economic woes. In other words, the Nazis framed themselves as a much more optimistic party, captivating young minds with an exciting sense of purpose.

In 1933, the nationwide book burnings shed light on how much popular support the Nazis had amongst students. Indeed, this infamous event was organized by the German Student Association, which wanted to cleanse academia of books that contradicted the principles of National Socialism. This included books by Jews, liberals, pacifists, and foreigners.

During the book burning in Berlin, Goebbels addressed the assembled students, calling upon them to be courageous in the face of death and embrace the new spirit of Germany. Similar book burnings took place across the country, most notably in towns and cities with universities.

Just like the students they taught, many of the professors were frustrated by the failings of the Weimar Republic and welcomed the Nazi takeover. Those few professors who did oppose the politics of the Third Reich risked losing their jobs. Jewish professors were simply dismissed from their posts.

The Night of Broken Glass

The Night of Broken Glass was another key event that demonstrated the ideological hold the Nazis had over young people. It took place on the 9th of November 1938, with the violence carrying through to the next day.

The event was designed to look like a spontaneous outburst against the Jewish community, but it was actually coordinated by

The KKK Flourished Under Prohibition

On this day in 1933, the Twenty-first Amendment to the United States Constitution was passed, repealing Prohibition. People around the country celebrated Repeal Day, up to and including president Franklin Delano Roosevelt, who received a case of Budweiser carried by the company's famous draft horses. But one group had little reason to celebrate: the Ku Klux Klan, which had allied itself with Prohibition campaigners intent on "purifying" the country–and prospered as a result.

Speaking to *Slate*'s Rebecca Onion, historian Lisa McGirr said that the resurgence of the Ku Klux Klan in the 1920s was related to the passage of the Volstead Act, which imposed Prohibition, in 1920. When she looked at how the hate group gathered members, she said, "it was often around the issue of the lack of observance of Prohibition, the issue of bootlegging, of cleaning up communities." However, these concerns masked other ones, she explained. "This issue was used instrumentally as a mandate to target those groups they already saw as enemies of white Protestant nationalism: immigrants, Catholics and African Americans."

The Ku Klux Klan's support of Prohibition gave the organization a way to promote its views and a way to perpetrate state-sanctioned violence against people of color, Catholics and Jews. "The war on the Nazi Party. With the help of the Brownshirts (the paramilitary wing of the Nazi Party), the Hitler Youth attacked buildings belonging to the Jewish community, such as synagogues and Jewish-owned businesses. They even desecrated cemeteries and broke into Jewish homes.

The emergency services did nothing to stop the violence, allowing members of the Hitler Youth to continue their destruction. Around 1,000 synagogues were burned or damaged, and 7,500 businesses were looted and ransacked. Thousands of Jewish men were arrested and taken to concentration

alcohol united Progressives and Protestants, federal agents and Klansmen," writes Kelefa Sanneh for *The New Yorker*.

The American government created an entire Prohibition Bureau intended to enforce alcohol-free living. However, this bureau selectively targeted groups that were perceived as inherently corrupt, like poor people, immigrants, and African Americans. Remember, the Jazz Age unfolded during Prohibition–plenty of people were drinking plenty of liquor.

The collaboration didn't end there. The underresourced Prohibition Bureau's agents "sometimes increased their ranks by deputizing volunteers, including members of the Ku Klux Klan, who found the battle to enforce Prohibition consistent with their broader mission to purify the nation," writes Sanneh. "In 1923, in Williamson County, Illinois, hundreds of enforcers, many of them Klansmen, began a series of violent raids on distilleries, bars, and private homes, in which several hundred people were arrested and more than a dozen were killed."

In the end, Prohibition didn't "purify" the nation by stopping drinking. What it did do was foster a nationwide climate of turmoil, and this was great for organizations that benefited from people's fears and anxieties–like the Klan. McGirr argues that the politics of Prohibition paved the way for today's far-right nationalist movements–just one example of its long reach.

"Why the Ku Klux Klan Flourished Under Prohibition" by Smithsonian Magazine, December 5, 2017.

camps. Those Jews who remained had to clear up the rubble without assistance.

The Night of Broken Glass was a watershed moment. In the wake of the event, the Nazis passed anti-Semitic laws, enforcing the transfer of Jewish-owned properties to Aryans. Other laws barred Jews from employment and public transport. Jewish children were also removed from schools.

Young Resistance Groups in Nazi Germany

Youth groups outside of Nazi influence, far from growing in size, stopped altogether. Catholic groups, for example, were disbanded in 1939, and music groups also suffered following the boycott of all organizations that didn't align with National Socialism.

However, some young people did fight back against the Nazis. At Munich University, a student organization known as White Rose opposed the fascist regime. Formed in 1942, the organization consisted of a group of students and a professor who rebelled against the Nazis by distributing leaflets. These leaflets highlighted the crimes of the Nazi Party and urged people to resist.

Other notable resistance groups included the Leipzig Meuten, a communist-inspired group, and the Edelweiss Pirates, who went out and picked physical fights with the Hitler Youth. Being a member of these organizations was risky, as it could result in being arrested by the Gestapo and imprisoned in a concentration camp.

Denazification After World War II

The speed at which the Nazis managed to implement these changes was frightening. They were only in power for twelve years, yet they completely revolutionized the education of young people by Nazifying schools and creating fascistic youth organizations.

Thankfully, these changes were not permanent. Under Allied occupation, the denazification process filtered through every aspect of Germany. But not everyone was pleased about these changes. Young people who remembered the economic woes of the Weimar Republic protested against democratization.

At the same time, they couldn't ignore the failings of the Third Reich. The revolutionary principles promoted by the Nazis appeared hollow and deceptive after Germany's loss in the Second World War. Young people, far from being politically active, became increasingly disillusioned with political affairs once the Nazis had been defeated.

Viewpoint 3

> *"Social media and other media can be positive influences on pre-teen and teenage behaviour and attituds. Media messages can have a negative or unhealthy influence on pre-teen and teenage behaviour and attitudes in certain areas, including self-image, body image, health and citizenship."*

Pre-teens and Teens Can Think about What They See in the Media

Raising Children Network

In the following viewpoint, Raising Children Network maintains that social media and influencers have both positive and negative effects on teens and pre-teens. Raising Children network promotes working with children to help them become savvy consumers of media, and they offer concrete suggestions for coaching teens and pre-teens to manage their media consumption. Raising Children Network is a site funded by the Australian Government which provides expert, up-to-date advice on parenting.

As you read, consider the following questions:

1. According to the author, what are three ways that media affect children negatively?

2. According to the author, what are three ways that media affect children positively?
3. As stated by the viewpoint, what kinds of questions should teens and pre-teens ask of media and media influencers?

Pre-teens and teenagers can be smart consumers of media messages. They don't just take in everything they see and hear on social media or in other media. You can help them develop the skills they need to handle media influence.

Media influence on pre-teens and teenagers can be deliberate and direct. For example, advertising is often directed at children of all ages. This means that children, pre-teens and teenagers are increasingly conscious of brands and images.

Media influence can also be indirect. For example, this might include sexualised images and content on Instagram, Snapchat, TikTok, YouTube and Twitch. It might also include violent imagery and coarse language in news media, documentaries, video games and song lyrics. This kind of media influence can suggest to pre-teens and teenagers that certain ways of behaving and looking are 'normal'.

Positive social media and other media influences on pre-teens and teenagers

Social media and other media can be positive influences on pre-teen and teenage behaviour and attitudes.

Citizenship

Pre-teens and teenagers who are exposed to and take an interest in news media are more likely to be interested in major social and political issues like climate change. Media can encourage them to become more involved as citizens in their communities or to connect with others on issues they feel strongly about.

Health and lifestyle

Pre-teens and teenagers can also pick up important health promotion messages from social media and other media. This might include messages aimed at preventing youth depression and suicide, promoting positive, respectful relationships, or encouraging healthy eating and lifestyle habits.

Identity

Good-quality stories in TV shows and movies can help pre-teens and teenagers explore aspects of identity like sexuality, relationships, gender or ethics. Examples include the treatment of sexuality in a TV show like *Heartstopper*, relationships in the TV show *Heartbreak High*, gender in the movies *Ride Like a Girl* and *Barbie*, or ethics in a TV show like *The Good Place*. These shows and movies can spark interesting and helpful conversations when you watch them with your child at an appropriate age.

Negative social media and other media influences on pre-teens and teenagers

Media messages can have a negative or unhealthy influence on pre-teen and teenage behaviour and attitudes in certain areas, including self-image, body image, health and citizenship.

Self-image and body image

Your child's self-image and body image can be influenced by social media, other media and advertising. For example, if your child regularly sees staged and filtered images on social media, they might feel they're not good enough. Or if your child sees unrealistic 'thin' or 'muscly' body types often enough, it can affect their body image and eating behaviour. These images can be even more powerful when there's no-one to disagree with messages like 'Thin is beautiful'.

Health and lifestyle

Social media and other media can influence the decisions that pre-teens and teenagers make about their health and lifestyle. For example, media messages and content can make it look 'normal', cool or grown up to eat or not eat [a] particular food, to smoke, vape, drink alcohol or take other drugs, to do unrealistic or unproven health regimes, or to gamble.

Citizenship

To be responsible citizens, pre-teens and teenagers need reliable and good-quality information. But social media and other media are sometimes used in negative ways during elections and at other times. For example, fake news or deepfakes might influence your child to believe misinformation or disinformation about a politician, public figure or celebrity. Online forums might also promote biased or hateful attitudes.

How media celebrities and influencers influence pre-teens and teenagers

Celebrities and influencers can be powerful influences on pre-teens and teenagers.

Pre-teens and teenagers can be attracted to lifestyles, products or behaviour that celebrities and influencers promote on social media. This can sometimes be a negative influence—for example, YouTuber Logan Paul's risky behaviour or Mr Beast's questionable business practices. But there are many celebrities whose lifestyles, values and behaviour provide positive examples—for example, YouTuber Elise Ecklund.

Pre-teens and teenagers need to be aware that influencers and some celebrities are paid to advertise the products they endorse.

Helping pre-teens and teenagers handle media influence

Exposure to media messages is a part of modern life, but you can help your child work out what's worth paying attention to.

Talking about media messages

The best way to help your child navigate the influence of social media and other media is to talk about media messages. For example, if your child likes watching beauty channels on YouTube, you could talk about product advertising and sponsorship. Or if your child is into a computer game like Fortnite, you could talk about the violence and looting that occurs in the game.

Encouraging a questioning attitude

When you're talking about media with your child, you can encourage them to ask questions too. This can help your child sort facts from opinion, identify advertising and fake news, understand bias and be aware of the misuse of statistics.

For example, you could choose one of the YouTube channels or TikTok accounts your child follows. Ask your child:

- Who's behind it?
- What's their motivation? How can you tell?
- What do they want from you?
- How does it make you feel?
- Do they want you to feel that way? Why?

You can do the same for celebrities and influencers. Encourage your child to ask themselves:

- Why do I like these people?
- Are they presented in a realistic way?
- Are they like this in real life?
- What values does this person portray?
- How does this person make me feel about myself?
- Why is this person telling me about this product or activity?
- Are there signs that this person is an influencer?

During an election campaign, you and your child could look at political news and memes together. Encourage your child to ask:

- What ideas are being promoted in this news story or meme?
- Who wrote this story or made this meme and why?
- How might this meme influence voters during the election?
- What do ABC News Verify and AAP FactCheck say about this information?

Understanding advertising

You can help to limit the influence of advertising on your child by talking about how advertising sells ideas as well as products. For example, you could encourage your child to ask:

- Does this advertisement link the product with a particular kind of lifestyle?
- How does that make you feel about the product?
- What messages does this advertisement send about what people should look like, wear, do, eat and drink?

Participating in online forums or group chats

If your child spends a lot of time on online forums or online group chats like Reddit or Discord, it's good to get your child thinking about questions like these:

- What do people talk about on the forum?
- What are the forum's attitudes towards race, ethnicity, gender and sexuality? Are any of these attitudes biased or even hateful?
- Does the forum make you feel safe and happy or uncomfortable?
- Does it align with your own values or beliefs?

Children and teenagers sometimes need help to get out of negative forums and chats and find forums or chats that match their values. For example, if the negative forum is built into a game, you could suggest that your child takes a break from the game while you help them find a different game to play.

Helping teenagers balance the influence of social media and other media

When your child balances media use with other activities like physical and creative activities and face-to-face socialising, your child experiences a wide range of influences. These include peers, community mentors and family, as well as the media.

You can also introduce your child to real-life, positive role models. Ways to do this could be joining local community groups, sporting clubs or mentoring programs.

Viewpoint 4

> *"In part, voters are frustrated with the political establishment, but they also have concerns about globalisation, immigration, a dilution of national identity and the European Union."*

A Boom in Europe's Right Wing Political Parties

BBC News

In the following viewpoint, BBC News maintains that voters in Europe are particularly attuned to certain problems that they perceive to plague their countries. BBC News analyzes 12 different European countries and the contentious issues in each. BBC News is one of the world's leading public broadcasting news services and is based in the UK.

As you read, consider the following questions:

1. Which political parties appear to be having a boom in Europe, according to the BBC?
2. What is a common target of dislike of many Europeans, as stated by BBC News?
3. How is the right-wing party in Poland different than others, as reported by the viewpoint?

Nationalism has always been a feature across Europe's political spectrum but there has been a recent boom in voter support for right-wing and populist parties.

It is visible from Germany, where the AfD has become the biggest opposition party in the Bundestag, to Spain, where Vox has become the third largest force in parliament.

In part, voters are frustrated with the political establishment, but they also have concerns about globalisation, immigration, a dilution of national identity and the European Union.

In the European Parliament, nine far-right parties have formed a new bloc, called Identity and Democracy (ID).

So where in Europe's political landscape do right-wing nationalists hold sway?

Italy

Italy's Matteo Salvini—leader of the League—is a key figure in Europe's nationalist scene, despite the collapse of his ruling coalition with the anti-establishment Five Star Movement in August.

A surprise deal between Five Star and the centre-left Democratic Party (PD) ended Mr Salvini's tenure as interior minister.

The League's popularity coincided with the aftermath of the financial crisis and a big influx of sub-Saharan migrants from North Africa in 2016. As interior minister, Mr Salvini spearheaded an anti-immigration policy that barred humanitarian rescue ships from Italian ports.

His party has long had a Eurosceptic reputation. It is leading the Italian opinion polls and has 28 MEPs in the new EU Parliament's 73-strong ID bloc.

Germany

In 2017 the far-right Alternative for Germany (AfD) entered the federal parliament for the first time with 12.6% of the vote, becoming Germany's biggest opposition party.

From its beginnings as an anti-euro party, it has pushed for strict anti-immigration policies, embraced hostility towards

Islam and broken decades-old anti-Nazi taboos. It enjoyed a surge in popularity as Germany allowed in over a million undocumented migrants.

Despite attempts by Chancellor Angela Merkel to toughen her stance on immigration, the party has added to its electoral success and now has representatives in every state parliament.

In October 2019 the AfD came ahead of Mrs Merkel's Christian Democrats (CDU) in the eastern state of Thuringia—a shock to the political establishment.

The AfD is strongest in ex-communist eastern Germany. Its supporters chant "Wir sind das Volk!" (We are the People)—an emotive slogan from the anti-communist protests of 1989.

The AfD is also Eurosceptic and Nigel Farage, leader of the UK's Brexit Party, took part in its 2017 election campaign.

The Brexit Party was the clear winner in the UK's European elections in May, despite its lack of seats in the UK Parliament. The party insists that the UK must leave the EU unconditionally: it argues that this was mandated by the Leave vote in the UK's 2016 referendum.

Spain

One of the big political stories in Spain has been the sudden rise of the far-right Vox party.

Spain held its fourth general election in four years on 10 November and Vox surged into third place, doubling its seats to 52. It only entered parliament for the first time in April.

Vox styles itself as defending the unity of the Spanish state, with a promise to deport illegal immigrants and repeal laws against gender violence.

It has made major gains by calling for a suspension of autonomy for the north-eastern Catalonia region, after separatists failed in their push for independence in October 2017.

Many believed that Spaniards would never endorse a far-right party due to its history under dictator Francisco Franco, who died in 1975. Just a single seat had been won by a far-right candidate since then—in 1979.

Austria

The Freedom Party (FPÖ) became the only far-right party in power in Western Europe when it joined a coalition as junior partner with conservative Chancellor Sebastian Kurz in 2017. His People's Party, along with the centre-left Social Democrats, have long dominated Austrian politics.

As in Germany, the migrant crisis that unfolded in 2015 was also seen as key to the FPÖ's success, and an issue they long campaigned on.

During its time in power the Freedom Party became caught up in a series of race rows. Then, party leader Heinz-Christian Strache and parliament group head Johann Gudenus were caught up in a scandal over a video "sting" filmed in Ibiza in 2017.

Mr Strache resigned and the fallout led to the far-right party quitting the government and support for the FPÖ fell sharply to 16% in September elections.

France

Despite the efforts of leader Marine Le Pen to make the far right palatable to France's mainstream, she was comprehensively defeated by Emmanuel Macron for the presidency in May 2017.

Her National Front (FN) failed to break through in parliamentary elections the following month, and the party was then renamed the National Rally (Rassemblement National).

Ms Le Pen's party is opposed to the euro and blames the EU for mass immigration, and she has found a common voice with other nationalist and far-right parties in Europe.

There is evidence that the grassroots "gilets jaunes" (yellow-vest) protest movement has attracted some activists from the far right.

The anti-establishment protests over the cost of living have posed probably the biggest challenge to the Macron presidency.

Some gilets jaunes protesters include anti-Semitic abuse in their angry campaign.

Sweden

The anti-immigration Sweden Democrats (SD) made significant gains in the 2018 general election, winning about 18% of the vote.

The party has its roots in neo-Nazism, but it rebranded itself in recent years and first entered parliament in 2010. It opposes multiculturalism and wants strict immigration controls.

As with many of the countries featured here, though, the picture is complex. Sweden has welcomed more asylum seekers per capita than any other European country and has one of the most positive attitudes towards migrants.

Finland

The far-right Finns Party were narrowly beaten into second place in the April 2019 general election, coming within 0.2% of the left-wing Social Democratic Party (SDP).

Its success was built on two policies: opposition to immigration and a rejection of ambitious policies aimed at combating climate change.

It was an extraordinary recovery for a party that had also done well in the previous vote in 2015 but had since faded in popularity because of party splits.

Estonia

Estonia's far-right Conservative People's Party of Estonia (EKRE) won its first seats in parliament in the 2015 election.

Four years later, EKRE has more than doubled its share of the vote to nearly 18%, making it the third-largest party. It used that power to negotiate a place in government, as it joined fellow runners-up the Centre and Pro Patria parties to stop liberal leader Kaja Kallas from becoming Estonia's first woman prime minister.

EKRE campaigned on an anti-immigration platform, and is also critical of same-sex marriage. Its leader, Martin Helme, once said that only white people should be allowed to move to Estonia.

"The Great Replacement" Is a Myth

The "great replacement theory," whose origins date back to the late 19th century, argues that Jews and some Western elites are conspiring to replace white Americans and Europeans with people of non-European descent, particularly Asians and Africans.

The conspiracy evolved from a series of false ideas that, over time, stoked the fears of white people: In 1892, British-Australian author and politician Charles Pearson warned that white people would "wake to find ourselves elbowed and hustled, and perhaps even thrust aside by people whom we looked down." The massive influx of immigrants into Europe at the time fostered some of these fears and resulted in "white extinction anxiety." In the U.S., it resulted in policies targeting immigration in the late 19th and early 20th century.

In France, journalist Édouard Drumont, leader of an antisemitic movement, wrote articles in the late 19th century imagining how Jews would destroy French culture. In 1909, Filippo Tommaso Marinetti, an Italian poet and supporter of Benito Mussolini, argued that war and fascism were the only cure for the world. Fascism, then and now, worked to ensure white dominance.

This was followed by the eugenics movement, an erroneous and racist theory that supported forced sterilization of Black people, the mentally ill and other marginalized groups, who were all deemed "unfit."

The 1978 book entitled "The Turner Diaries," a fictional futuristic account of the overthrow of the United States government, further contributed to white nationalist ideas.

Collectively, these gave rise to a global movement that attracted a wide range of white supremacist, xenophobic and anti-immigration conspiracy theories. These theories were formally codified in the work of Frenchman Renaud Camus, first in his 2010 book "L'Abécédaire de l'in-nocence" and elaborated in his 2011 book "Le Grand Remplacement."

Camus argued that ethnic French and white Europeans were being replaced physically, culturally and politically by nonwhite people. He believed that liberal immigration policies and the dramatic decline in white birth rates were threatening European civilization and traditions.

Why this conspiracy theory matters

These false ideas promulgated the spread of white supremacy, which has contributed to terrorist attacks, state violence and propaganda campaigns in the U.S and parts of Europe.

On Aug. 11, 2017, during a "Unite the Right" rally in Charlottesville, Virginia, white nationalists chanted "You will not replace us" and "Jews will not replace us." In spring 2019, Belgian politician Dries Van Langenhove repeatedly posted on social media, "We are being replaced."

In recent years, nonwhite immigrants have been the target of xenophobia. Migrants, especially from Mexico, are accused of bringing criminal activities to American cities. Immigrants have also been falsely accused of smuggling fentanyl into the U.S. The reality is that immigrants commit far fewer crimes than those born in the U.S.

Impact of the theory and spread of hate

In less than two decades, the theory has become a major idea, with as many as 60% of the French population believing some aspects of it. According to that survey, they are worried or at least concerned that they might be replaced. In the U.K. and the U.S., close to one-third of those polled believe that white people are systematically being replaced by nonwhite immigrants. Some in the U.S. fear that America might lose its culture and identity as a result.

Being aware of conspiracy theories and standing up to hatred, I argue, can help societies deal with the continuing fallout of extreme xenophobia, racist rants, the rise of white supremacy and the victimization of innocent people.

"What is the 'great replacement theory'? A scholar of race relations explains" by Rodney Coates, *The Conversation*, March 15, 2024.

Poland

The far-right Confederation party got 6.8% of the vote in Poland's 2019 general election.

But the main story of the election was the convincing win for conservative Law and Justice (PiS), returning to power with 43.6% of the vote.

PiS is led by a veteran anti-communist campaigner, Jaroslaw Kaczynski, whose bedrock support is in rural Poland, with its deep-rooted Catholic traditions. The party is strong on social welfare, as well as nationalism, making it rather different from many other right-wing parties in Europe.

The PiS government's controversial overhaul of Poland's judiciary has put it in dispute with the EU Commission.

Hungary

In 2018, Hungarian Prime Minister Viktor Orban secured a third term in office with a landslide victory in an election dominated by immigration.

The victory, he said, gave Hungarians "the opportunity to defend themselves and to defend Hungary".

Mr Orban has long presented himself as the defender of Hungary and Europe against Muslim migrants, once warning of the threat of "a Europe with a mixed population and no sense of identity".

In March 2019 Europe's mainstream centre-right grouping, the EPP, suspended Fidesz because of its anti-EU stance.

Hungary has two nationalist parties—with Jobbik attempting to escape its far-right past and appeal to centrist voters—and gaining 19% of the vote in 2018.

Slovenia

Although it fell a long way short of a majority, the anti-immigrant Slovenian Democratic Party (SDS) was the largest party in this year's general election.

The party is led by former Prime Minister Janez Jansa, a supporter of Hungary's Viktor Orban. He has said he wants Slovenia to "become a country that will put the wellbeing and security of Slovenians first".

Greece

An anti-immigration, nationalist party called Greek Solution got 3.7% in Greece's 2019 national election, giving it 10 seats in the 300-seat parliament.

The neo-Nazi Golden Dawn party no longer has any seats in the parliament.

Voter frustration with Greece's continuing economic malaise and the migrant crisis has not translated into a big surge for the far right.

> *"April is also Genocide Awareness Month. Holocaust Remembrance Day takes place this month every year, as do commemorations for genocides in Cambodia, Iraqi Kurdistan, Rwanda, Bosnia and Darfur."*

A Spotlight on Those Who Resist Hate

Nareg Seferian

In the following viewpoint, Nareg Seferian notes that hate and genocide are not new occurrences, but they sometimes reappear in new ways. Seferian dissects several instances of historical acts of hate and genocide, while providing modern day research that has documented the resistance efforts before, during, and after the instances of hate and genocide. Nareg Seferian is an academic working in the school of public and international affairs at Virginia Tech. His area of expertise focuses on the country of Armenia.

As you read, consider the following questions:

1. What is new surrounding incidents of genocide, according to this author?
2. According to Seferian, what role do books and stories play in incidents of genocide?

"Genocide resisters, long overlooked by history, step into the spotlight" by Nareg Sefarian, *The Conversation*, April 24, 2023.

3. As reported by this viewpoint, how can fictional works play a role in anti-genocide action?

The anniversary of the Armenian Genocide is marked every year on April 24. That was the date in 1915 when hundreds of Armenian community leaders were arrested by the government of the Ottoman Empire in the capital Constantinople, now known as Istanbul.

At the time, Armenians lived throughout what is modern-day Turkey. Modern scholars estimate up to 1.5 million Armenians were killed by the Turkish government, and around 800,000 to 1.2 million were deported during World War I. Most ended up in the Middle East, the Caucasus, Russia, Europe and the Americas. During that period, Greek, Assyrian and Yezidi communities were also massacred and forced to flee into exile.

April is also Genocide Awareness Month. Holocaust Remembrance Day takes place this month every year, as do commemorations for genocides in Cambodia, Iraqi Kurdistan, Rwanda, Bosnia and Darfur.

For much of the 20th century, commemorations of mass killings and genocide have focused on remembering the dead as victims and condemning the perpetrators.

But recent research has taken a broader view, recognizing that mass violence takes place because of many complex factors. Besides political, economic and cultural currents, the resistance and resilience of the people who were targeted are coming to the fore of scholarly work and public understanding.

1909 before 1915

The 1915 Armenian Genocide was not the first attack on Armenians in what is now Turkey. In the 1890s, hundreds of thousands of Armenians were targeted by the government of the Ottoman Empire in what came to be called the Hamidian Massacres, as they took place during the reign of Sultan Abdul Hamid II.

And in 1909—again, in April—there was a separate such episode. Those massacres took place in the region historically known as Cilicia, on the Mediterranean coast of southeastern Turkey today. In two waves of violence at the end of April 1909, more than 20,000 Armenians and other Christians were killed by Turks connected with the government. The violence happened in and around the city of Adana and extended into neighboring areas. Muslim populations suffered as well, with an estimated 2,000 killed in retaliation for the massacres.

Some present the Hamidian and Adana massacres as dress rehearsals for the Ottoman Turkish government's plan, decades in the making, to implement the all-out elimination of the Armenians in 1915, dispossessing them of their millennia-old historical homeland. Among Armenians, this is the prevalent nationalist reading of Armenian history.

Survivors on their own terms

Recent scholarship has taken a closer look at the details of these massacres. In particular, scholars are beginning to highlight the fact that, despite facing mass violence, Armenians and others organized resistance activities and put together relief work in the aftermath of killings. Sometimes resistance was armed, and sometimes it consisted of putting together protest campaigns or publishing newspaper articles and books in the Ottoman Empire and beyond.

"The Horrors of Adana" by Bedross Der Matossian is the first in-depth work on the Adana Massacres. Der Matossian writes about the actions of a prominent literary figure, Zabel Yessayan, who was among the leaders of relief efforts following the 1909 massacres, bringing in food, clothing and other necessities for the survivors. Yessayan also wrote "In The Ruins," published in 1911, specifically to document the aftermath of the killings and to support humanitarian aid, media outreach and legal efforts.

"The Resistance Network" by Khatchig Mouradian documents the work of Armenian community leaders such as Rev. Aharon Shirajian to support the survivors of death marches and deportations. Shirajian himself cared for a number of orphaned genocide survivors in Syria.

These stories are not only powerful on their own but can also have lasting effects in the global effort to end genocide. Fiction can play a role, too. "The Forty Days of Musa Dagh" by Franz Werfel is a gripping novel that recounts the armed defense by a group of Armenians in one corner of the Ottoman Empire in 1915.

The book, which was published in 1933, the year Hitler took power, served as an inspiration for the anti-Nazi resistance in the Jewish ghettos of Warsaw, Bialystok, Vilnius and elsewhere in the 1940s.

Jewish resistance to the Nazi genocide is another topic being given due attention by historians. The book "Resisters" by Wolf Gruner is a work along these lines, focusing on the actions of five Jewish individuals during the Holocaust.

These efforts are beginning to shift how scholars and the public understand genocide. Those horrific actions were not carried out against passive victims, but rather were aggressions which, in many cases, faced intense and organized resistance. The perpetrators killed many but did not destroy the spirit of their victims. The survivors and their descendants have good reason to celebrate that spirit of resilience in the face of immense suffering.]

Periodical and Internet Sources Bibliography

The following articles have been selected to supplement the diverse views presented in this chapter.

David Bauder, "What is 'Great Replacement Theory' and How Does It Fuel Racist Violence?" PBS News, May 16, 2022. www.pbs.org/newshour/politics/what-is-great-replacement-theory-and-how-does-it-fuel-racist-violence.

Paul J. Becker, "Replacement Theory Isn't New-3 Things to Know About How This Once-Fringe Conspiracy Has Become More Mainstream," *University of Dayton Magazine*, May 25, 2022. udayton.edu/magazine/2022/05/replacement-theory.php.

Shelby Dioum, "What Explains the Increase in Online Hate Speech," UCDavis, March 4, 2025. www.ucdavis.edu/magazine/what-explains-increase-online-hate-speech.

Emily Ekins, "82% Say It's Hard to Ban Hate Speech Because People Can't Agree What Speech Is Hateful," CATO Institute, November 8, 2017. www.cato.org/blog/82-say-its-hard-ban-hate-speech-because-people-cant-agree-what-speech-hateful.

John F. Fisher, "The Culture of Hate," Scientific Research, July 2024. www.scirp.org/journal/paperinformation?paperid=134386.

Lulu Garcia-Navarro, "What is White Replacement Theory? Explaining the White Supremacist Rhetoric," NPR, September 26, 2021. www.npr.org/2021/09/26/1040756471/what-is-white-replacement-theory-explaining-the-white-supremacist-rhetoric.

Marie Gettel-Gilmartin, "Normalizing Hate Speech is Not Cultural Progress," LinkedIn, May 12, 2025. www.linkedin.com/pulse/normalizing-hate-speech-cultural-progress-marie-gettel-gilmartin-iuwvc/.

Anya Kamenetz, "Right-Wing Hate Groups Are Recruiting Video Gamers," NPR, November 5, 2018. www.npr.org/2018/11/05/660642531/right-wing-hate-groups-are-recruiting-video-gamers.

Matt Schiavenza, "Deep Dive: The Great Replacement Theory," HIAS, November 1, 2024. hias.org/news/deep-dive-great-replacement-theory/.

Jason Wilson, "The Racist 'Great Replacement' Conspiracy Theory," Southern Poverty Law Center, May 17, 2022. www.splcenter.org/resources/hatewatch/racist-great-replacement-conspiracy-theory-explained/.

OPPOSING VIEWPOINTS® SERIES

CHAPTER 4

Can Hate Speech and Hate Groups Be Prevented in the Future?

Chapter Preface

Hate and violence may have ancient roots and have evolved into modern times, but can hate speech and violence be prevented in the future? This final chapter examines several ways that hate speech and the violence that often ensues might be avoided.

One viewpoint author delves into the human virtue of tolerance. Can a person's capacity for tolerance be taught in schools and universities? Could this prevent children and young adults from growing up with preconceived notions of hate and the tendency toward violence? A few other viewpoint articles examine the role that social media plays with respect to hate speech and violence. How should social media sites change? Should the CEOs of social media conglomerates care about users, or do they only have to please their stockholders?

Two extremely contentious issues are also discussed by the viewpoint authors in this chapter. One is about the connection between gun ownership and violence, and the other is about the debate surrounding Confederate statues in the United States. Do the statues play a role in the continuation of white supremacy and racial hate and division? Does high gun ownership contribute to the rate of gun violence?

While there may never be a clear answer to the question of whether hate and violence can be solved, reading, debate, and understanding of the issues presented in this final chapter can help people formulate ideas that get us closer to that goal.

Community Policing Increases Public Trust

A new EU-funded project aims to support community policing by focusing on small, decentralized police units that work closely with local communities. In response to Europe's rapidly evolving demographic, technological, and economic landscape, the project integrates reactive, proactive, and co-active policing approaches, empowering law enforcement to engage effectively with socially complex environments.

Europe's societal landscape is rapidly evolving due to ongoing demographic, technological, and economic transformations. These changes have introduced new complexities to public safety and community cohesion, pushing law enforcement agencies (LEAs) to adapt their approach to policing. Communities are becoming more diverse and interconnected—both physically and digitally—presenting unprecedented challenges in crime prevention, security, and public trust.

Traditional policing methods are revealing to be limited in addressing the multifaceted needs of modern, non-homogeneous societies. Concerns such as radicalisation, hate crimes, and the digitalisation of criminal activity require law enforcement to adopt more adaptive, responsive, and collaborative strategies. At the same time, public trust in police forces remains fragile, making community engagement and transparency critical components of modern policing.

Introducing KOBAN: A new vision for community policing

The KOBAN project was launched to support community policing by focusing on small, decentralised police units that collaborate closely with local communities. By integrating reactive, proactive, and co-active policing approaches, the project addresses diverse societal challenges, including radicalisation and crime prevention, through an ethical, legal, and culturally aware framework. The goal is to empower law enforcement to effectively engage with non-homogeneous, socially complex environments, both online and in-person.

The project officially kicked off with its initial meeting in Valencia (Spain), where consortium members from across Europe came together to outline the project's goals and strategies. This marked the beginning of an important journey towards reshaping community policing and establishing a model that is both adaptable and future-proof.

Enhancing digital interactions with AI-driven tools

KOBAN aims to revolutionise how police and civilians interact by delivering innovative, AI-powered digital communication tools. These tailor-made solutions are designed to build trust between police and communities, enhancing transparency and accountability. By offering advanced analysis of local crime patterns and improving real-time communication, KOBAN equips law enforcement with future-proof technologies that strengthen their ability to maintain public safety and address the needs of diverse populations.

Tailored training for law enforcement and community partners

To prepare police officers and community stakeholders for the complexities of modern society, KOBAN will implement a modular training program. This program will focus on balancing the needs of majority groups while ensuring the inclusion of minority and vulnerable populations. The training emphasises practical skills for working within socially diverse settings, supporting both police and community actors in applying community policing strategies effectively across Europe.

Driving cultural and organisational change

KOBAN's capability-driven approach will not only develop cutting-edge tools and training but also lead a cultural and organisational transformation within law enforcement agencies. By providing a comprehensive, adaptable framework for community policing, KOBAN ensures that these innovative solutions can be customised and widely adopted by local police forces across Europe. This framework addresses the barriers to effective community policing, creating a foundation for sustainable, trust-based interactions between law enforcement and the public.

"Redefining community policing: Innovative solutions for modern challenges" by Innovative Prison Systems, October 4, 2024.

Viewpoint 1

> *"... schools and universities should deliberately widen the exposure of students and learners to a diversity of people and views. This will develop their capacities as democratic citizens and enhance the human quest for flourishing in everyday social life."*

Tolerance Can Reduce Hate

Nuraan Davids and Yusef Waghid

In the following viewpoint, Nuraan Davids and Yusef Waghid contend that schools and universities play a large role in the prevention of hate by teaching tolerance. Davids and Waghid provide definitions and examples of tolerance by quoting scholars and philosophers. Finally, the authors emphasize that teachers must lead students to understanding by exposing them to multiple perspectives. Nuraan Davids and Yusef Waghid are professors of educational philosophy at Stellenbosch University in South Africa.

As you read, consider the following questions:

1. According to the authors, how do schools and universities teach tolerance?
2. How do scholars and philosophers define tolerance, as reported by the viewpoint?

3. According to Davids and Waghid, what does tolerance allow people to do?

More and more, educational leaders and managers in schools and universities are being confronted with various expressions of hate speech.

In Cape Town, South Africa, a group of high school boys compiled a song which included the lyrics: "I feel pain unearthly because of my hatred of kaffirs". The word "kaffir" is an apartheid-era racial slur and possibly the most offensive word in the South African lexicon. At the University of Witwatersrand, also in South Africa, the phrase "Kill a Jew" was spray-painted on one of its main buildings.

Similarly, in the US, racist flyers were found posted on the campus of Weber State University in Utah. The flyers were recruiting students to the white supremacist Alt-Right movement and declared that "diversity is a code word for White genocide".

In May this year Stellenbosch University in South Africa became another example. Three students put up Nazi-inspired posters on campus advertising an "Anglo-Afrikaner student" event under the motto "Fight for Stellenbosch".

The incident caused a massive outcry and the university acted immediately and decisively to condemn the inflammatory hate speech. The students were found guilty of contravening the Student Disciplinary Code, which states that

> *A student shall not act in a manner that is racist, unfairly discriminatory, violent, grossly insulting, abusive or intimidating against any other person.*

Incidents like these bring to the fore the question of how institutions of learning can and should be responding to such controversies, which lay bare our simmering intolerance of difference and "otherness".

In our latest book, *Tolerance and Dissent within Education: On Cultivating Debate and Understanding*, we look at how the concept of tolerance might be understood, cultivated and enacted in and through education.

One of the arguments we make is that schools and universities should deliberately widen the exposure of students and learners to a diversity of people and views. This will develop their capacities as democratic citizens and enhance the human quest for flourishing in everyday social life.

What is tolerance?

Andrew Murphy, a scholar from Rutgers University, describes tolerance as

> *the self-restraint of not restricting or reducing the rights or autonomy of others, or other ways of being and acting.*

But in a global context of heightened bigotry, some people see an appeal to tolerance as a defence of hate speech or racism. This is not what tolerance is. All views and actions should only be tolerated to the extent that they don't harm others—physically, psychologically or emotionally.

According to the classical Greek philosopher Socrates, tolerance is about the pursuit of truth. It is about being prepared to see the value of another person's perspective or truth. This necessarily means humbling oneself and acknowledging one's own limitations and fallibility. Tolerance, then, is fundamentally about equality; about recognising the capacity for both moral truth and error in ourselves and others.

Amy Gutmann from the University of Pennsylvania describes tolerance as

> *agreeing to disagree about beliefs and practices that are a matter of basic liberty.*

This, she argues, is a way to ensure larger civic participation of people, who are recognised as equals by their fellow citizens.

Simply put, tolerance is the choice to "agree to disagree" because we respect each other as moral and civic equals.

Difference, democracy and human flourishing

Whenever diverse communities of people come together there is the potential for peaceful coexistence as well as for conflict. If we were to all agree on what to think or how to act the need for tolerance would disappear. But we don't. So exercising tolerance is an acknowledgement of difference and disagreement—and, at the same time, a decision to co-exist despite these differences, rather than destroy them or each other.

This is fundamental to democracy, which is about equality and the right of people to believe what they believe. Agreement or consensus may be a desired end—if only to resolve conflict—but it is not a democratic imperative. Tolerance is the tool that helps us democratically manage the dynamics of any plural community or society.

But the value of tolerance goes beyond that. In protecting and cultivating diversity, tolerance also creates the conditions for human flourishing. Disagreement and dissent can be seen as processes of "mutual incitement". When people disagree, they are in fact inciting each other to think anew and differently about established ideas or beliefs. It is through disagreement that we dislodge ourselves from rigid ways of thinking and being—and refine our ideas and positions.

The responsibilities of schools and universities

Schools and universities must make sure that students and learners are exposed to multiple perspectives and ways of doing things. They have to encounter different viewpoints and arguments, and especially those that disrupt their own ways of thinking and their ideas of the world.

It is important that the teacher's worldview isn't the only one propagated in the classroom. This means teaching in a way such that pupils or students are invited to bring their own identities and equal intelligence into the conversation. They must be encouraged to engage in deliberation and debate, with mutual respect.

Education Gets at the Roots of Hate

Michael Georg Link, Director of the OSCE Office for Democratic Institutions and Human Rights (ODIHR), Michael O'Flaherty, Director of the EU Agency for Fundamental Rights (FRA), and Christian Ahlund, Chair of the Council of Europe's European Commission against Racism and Intolerance (ECRI), stressed that it is the responsibility of all, and political leaders in particular, to counter intolerant discourse and hate speech, and to ensure their root causes are addressed through education.

"We all play a crucial role in promoting mutual respect and inclusion, ensuring that we live in societies that foster respect for the rights and dignity of every person, regardless of their ethnicity, gender, religion or belief or any other identity," said ODIHR Director Link. "Political and community leaders have a greater responsibility, and must address intolerance in all its forms, so as to effectively counter hate speech, which can lead to violence and hate crimes and dangerously undermine security and social cohesion."

FRA Director O'Flaherty noted that hate speech is not limited to extremists, and that the deliberate manipulation of information designed to promote intolerance is squarely in the mainstream of political rhetoric. He stressed that these fabrications could only be countered through education and media literacy.

"The challenge is to address those who are receptive to intolerant views. Encouraging greater media literacy is an essential element of this, particularly in the digital environment," the FRA Director said. "We need to support both children and adults to critically assess what they see and hear in the media. This will enable them to recognise propaganda, and help them to confront and report statements that incite hatred."

In addition to the prompt condemnation of the use of hate speech, ECRI Chair Ahlund highlighted the need to challenge and engage those who propagate it.

"Policies against hate speech should also envisage steps to encourage those who use hate speech both to repudiate this use and to help them end their association with groups using it," he said. "This is not an easy task. Nonetheless, changing behaviours, by demonstrating both the falsity of the foundations on which hate speech is based and its unacceptability, is not impossible. Existing projects directed to this goal should be widely emulated and supported."

ODIHR, FRA and ECRI play an active role in countering hate speech, hate crime and other forms of intolerance. ODIHR reports on hate crimes across the OSCE's 57 participating States on hatecrime.osce.org and helps local authorities and civil society address this issue. FRA is developing a media toolkit to guide journalists on how to include a human rights perspective in their reporting. ECRI General Policy Recommendation No.15 contains guidelines on how to combat the use of hate speech and the No Hate Speech Movement is a youth campaign of the Council of Europe mobilising young people to act on hate speech and counter it.

The United Nations designated 21 March the International Day for the Elimination of Racial Discrimination in 1966, in memory of the 69 people killed six years earlier in Sharpeville, South Africa, during a peaceful demonstration to protest the apartheid system.

"Education to promote inclusion and mutual respect is essential to counter hate speech" by European Union Agency for Fundamental Rights, March 21, 2017.

Critical to any educative endeavour is an understanding that there is always the possibility of another perspective and, hence, disagreement. If educational institutions can protect learners from hate speech, whilst also successfully teaching them this this, they will prepare them to become both better democratic citizens and richer people.

Viewpoint 2

> *"To fix the dark side of platforms, only a combination of government regulation and pressure for companies to self-regulate has a chance to curb the extremes in social media."*

To Decrease Hate, Social Media Platforms Must Regulate Extreme Content

Michael A. Cusumano, David B. Yoffie, and Annabelle Gawer

In the following viewpoint, Michael A. Cusumano, David B. Yoffie, and Annabelle Gawer argue that in order to decrease hate, social media platforms must be made to regulate what proliferates on their sites. The authors present and analyze several options for forcing social media companies to comply. Michael A. Cusumano is a professor and dean at the MIT Sloan School of Management, David B. Yoffie is a professor at Harvard Business School, and Annabelle Gawer is a professor at Surrey Business School.

As you read, consider the following questions:

1. According to the authors, how does money prevent self-regulation by social media platforms?

"Pushing Social Media Platforms to Self-Regulate" by Michael A. Cusumano, David B. Yoffie and Annabelle Gawer, *The Regulatory Review*, January 3, 2022. Reprinted by Permission.

2. What goes against Facebook's community standards, as stated by the viewpoint?
3. What caused the movie and video game industry to regulate themselves, as reported by the viewpoint authors?

Online platforms can be "double-edged swords," generating spectacular economics while offering a forum for bad actors and bad behavior. To fix the dark side of platforms, only a combination of government regulation and pressure for companies to self-regulate has a chance to curb the extremes in social media. U.S. Supreme Court Justice Clarence Thomas has hinted at a similar position.

Although the challenges facing social media are global and require multinational solutions, we focus here mainly on the United States. We start by clarifying the problem we are trying to solve. On the one hand, social media platforms have an incentive problem. Facebook, Instagram, Google, YouTube, Twitter, and other platforms frequently accelerate the viral distribution of extreme content because it generates greater user engagement, which translates into billions of dollars in advertisements.

The more outrageous the content—for example, stories of grand conspiracies around the U.S. presidential election, the coronavirus, and COVID-19 vaccines—the greater the profit opportunity.

Yes, the social media companies have "terms of service" that allow them to delete harmful or illegal content. But there are no financial incentives for these firms to police themselves.

On the other hand, the volume of social media content—four billion videos are viewed on Facebook alone each day—makes it difficult and expensive, although not impossible, to track, curate, or edit so many postings.

We have been studying and writing about digital platforms since they first emerged in the 1990s. Our research has led us to conclude that many of the proposals being discussed in the press and the U.S. Congress are unlikely to work. Let us consider them one by one.

One option is to break up Facebook. This option would reduce Facebook's market power, but it does not solve any of the incentive problems or conflict of interest issues identified by Frances Haugen, the former Facebook employee and whistleblower. Even if Facebook, Instagram, and WhatsApp returned to separate companies, each application would still be a huge, powerful network with no new incentives to stop bad behavior. Similar problems would persist if YouTube were detached from Google.

Another option is for the federal government to regulate social media algorithms directly. This option, which Haugen proposed, is possible—but would be difficult to execute for technical reasons. Social media and search algorithms are designed using artificial intelligence technology. The algorithms are difficult for outsiders and even the software developers themselves to pull apart and alter, let alone fully understand. Furthermore, these algorithms are based on machine learning and big data. They continually evolve as users interact with the platforms billions of times a day. Putting in a bureaucratic change-control process monitored by government officials or even expert special masters—as occurred with the Microsoft antitrust trial settlement—would likely freeze the technology and put a damper on innovation.

A third option would be for lawmakers to eliminate Section 230. This change would get rid of the 1996 law that protects online platforms from civil liabilities for content they disseminate. But Section 230 distinguishes the platforms from publishers, the latter who are fully responsible for their content. As such, the law remains fundamental to the operations of all online platforms. We want these internet businesses to continue to be as open as possible to innovation and to facilitate freedom of expression in user-generated content—without being legally liable for each of the billions of posts on their sites.

A better alternative would be to combine government regulations that alter incentives and put more pressure on social media companies to do more self-regulation. We offer three suggestions.

First, the U.S. government should require all social media platforms to abide strictly by their own "terms of service," vesting enforcement power over these terms with the Federal Communications Commission (FCC), Federal Trade Commission (FTC), or even the Securities and Exchange Commission (SEC). These terms already give social media companies the ability to curate content or shut down accounts when they see misuse of their platforms. For example, Facebook has a set of "community standards" comprising a long list of potentially prohibited content, including posts considered to encourage violence and criminal behavior, child or sexual exploitation, hate speech, false news, and intellectual property violations.

Having terms of service is not enough, however. The federal government needs to make sure that social media firms adhere to their publicly stated terms of service and other standards. One way to force adherence would be government lawsuits or civil litigation—with fines levied against not only the companies, but also against their CEOs, other executives, and members of their boards of directors. Just as the Sarbanes-Oxley Act of 2002 made officers and directors personally liable for financial statements, new regulations could make Mark Zuckerberg and the Facebook board liable for failures to implement their terms of service.

Second, Congress, with the cooperation of the U.S. Department of Justice, should revise Section 230. We suggest that the revisions make it possible to hold the online platforms accountable for profits they earn from deliberately disseminating harmful content. The companies could then become open to civil lawsuits or specific FCC, FTC, SEC, or Justice Department actions. Since Facebook and Alphabet, Google's parent company, collectively earned $69 billion in net income in 2020, episodic fines are unlikely to alter behavior—as we have seen with European antitrust fines against Google or the $5 billion FTC fine levied against Facebook. It should be possible, however, to force the platforms to identify profits gained from advertisements tied to these viral posts and then to have those monies clawed back as fines. Those numbers could be very large.

Finally, any additional government regulation should be administered in a way that promotes more effective self-regulation, as occurred with movie ratings and advertisements for tobacco, alcohol, pornography, terrorist recruitment, or self-preferencing in airline flight listings during the 1960s and 1970s. The technology that digital platforms use is too complex and fast-changing, and the content too vast, to rely only on government monitoring.

Historically, when new, complex technologies arise and new industries emerge, a credible threat of intrusive government regulation triggers many companies to regulate their own operations. In industries such as movies and video games, the threat of government intervention spurred coalitions of firms to establish content standards and codes of conduct—including content rating systems—which have worked reasonably well. This coalition approach could work with social media platforms.

Ultimately, accountable self-regulation is good for business: Social media platforms need to take more responsibility for their impact on the world, lest they run the risk of continuing to damage essential common resources for information and commerce—the internet itself, and user trust in digital content.

VIEWPOINT 3

> *"... Facebook's real problem: its role in spreading disinformation and hate speech in communities around the world."*

Facebook Overstates Its Ability to Lessen the Spread of Hate Speech and Disinformation

Bhaskar Chakravorti

In the following viewpoint, Bhaskar Chakravorti analyzes the business practices of Facebook and how those practices prevent the company from lessening its impact on hate speech and disinformation. Charravorti contends that Mark Zuckerberg must work to please his companies' shareholders, and this makes it difficult to change social media. Bhaskar Chakravorti is a dean of global business at Tufts University and is a regular columnist for many publications, including Forbes, *the* Harvard Review, *and the* Washington Post.

As you read, consider the following questions:

1. As stated by the viewpoint, which of Zuckerberg's social media platforms makes the most money?
2. How do Zuckerberg's social media platforms make money, according to the author?

3. Which social media platform is causing violence and fear in India, as reported by Chakravorti?

Facebook's founder and CEO Mark Zuckerberg's latest promise is that his social media conglomerate will become a "privacy-focused" one. By turns lauded and lambasted, this move does not quite address users' primary problems with the company.

His move is the pragmatic shift of a CEO toward where the market is already headed. Ironically, Zuckerberg's announcement provides more evidence for Facebook critics who say the company doesn't understand even the concept of user privacy.

Zuckerberg has chosen an interesting metaphor to describe this change. He claims that people are shifting from publicly broadcasting their activities and views in a digital "town square"—and would rather discuss issues in a more secure, privacy-protective online "living room." His company already owns platforms representing both venues: Facebook is the town square, the largest platform for sharing widely, and WhatsApp is the living room, the largest platform for sharing in small groups.

As a former partner in McKinsey's strategy practice and now, as a scholar of strategy at Tufts' Fletcher School studying the effects of digital technologies in 80 countries, I have been analyzing Facebook's changing strategies for several years. I see Zuckerberg's latest move as Strategy 101: a market-driven shift of focus. That, by itself, is welcome. What is not so laudable is trying to package the move as a revolutionary solution to his company's widespread problems with privacy, facilitating fake news and underhand deals to share user data.

Worse, the changes will be difficult to execute and will not happen soon—or at least not soon enough for many users.

Driven by market forces

The writing is already on Zuckerberg's wall: Users are leaving the town square and filling living rooms. U.S. Facebook users' activity dropped in late 2018, while WhatsApp and Messenger activity grew.

Zuckerberg is merely preparing to shift resources to follow users from one platform to the other. However, Facebook's business model dictates that the company cannot make a true pivot away from the town square and toward the living room. As a publicly traded company, Zuckerberg has a fiduciary responsibility to shareholders to deliver returns on their investments. The town square makes all the money—and a lot of it.

Despite its troubles, Facebook made more money in 2018 than in previous years, and made more profit too. Most of the company's billions were generated by the town square version of Facebook.

Zuckerberg hasn't yet shown a plan for making the WhatsApp living room platform even remotely as profitable. Currently, his company makes 98 percent of its revenues from advertisers. It's had only limited success with advertisements in the Messenger app and hasn't even tested the concept in WhatsApp.

Moreover, the advertising revenue comes from companies that want to target the extensively detailed subgroups of Facebook's social network users. WhatsApp collects far less data and is encrypted, which means its users are harder to target as effectively.

Gradually shifting, not replacing

It may take Facebook a very long time to figure out how to make money from its shift to more private messaging.

A plan to integrate the technical infrastructure of WhatsApp and Messenger with Instagram would allow users to seamlessly communicate across three platforms for the first time. More importantly for Zuckerberg, though, it would link billions of detailed Facebook accounts with WhatsApp users—opening stockpiles of data to mine for advertisers.

The integration could save the company money by letting it consolidate servers that handle messaging—but there is still risk: It could raise the hackles of regulators. Technical consolidation could appear to be a preemptive move against calls to break up Facebook, including by prominent lawmakers, such as U.S. Sen. Elizabeth Warren.

Another possibility is that Facebook intends to adopt a business model more like China's immensely popular WeChat. WeChat makes money from commissions on mobile payments for a whole range of services within the app, including shopping, games, meal deliveries and even utility bills. Facebook is working on a new cryptocurrency and on handling payments through WhatsApp. But those efforts are in early stages—and late in the marketplace.

An essential facet of WeChat's business model is off-limits to Facebook. WeChat's parent company is widely believed to share user data with the Chinese government, in exchange for regulatory protection. That may be part of the political reality of China, but would doom Facebook in the Western markets it currently dominates.

A major problem still lingers in the living room

All of this talk about changing the business model ignores Facebook's real problem: its role in spreading disinformation and hate speech in communities around the world. Moving users' attention away from the town square—which needs to be monitored and moderated—to an encrypted, private living room is not a solution.

Private messaging might even make things worse. WhatsApp is already central to a trend of misinformation, fear and violence in India: Users passed the word from town to town that any strangers about might be there to kidnap children. More than 20 innocent people have been killed as a result of these terrifying—but false—rumors. WhatsApp has also been implicated in mob violence in Sri Lanka, and voter manipulation in Brazil and Nigeria.

The company has claimed it can do little about such falsehoods spreading, because they're encrypted and sent from user to user, rather than posted more publicly for others to view. Without addressing the problems of misinformation, shifting more communications to the living room will create more opportunities for fear, havoc and violence. This is especially true in the developing world, where users tend to be more trusting of digital media in general.

Zuckerberg also committed not to store data in countries with repressive governments, but that poses fresh problems. Many governments are discussing restrictions on free speech and data sharing, especially in countries where Facebook has some of the highest numbers of users, including India, Brazil, Indonesia, Vietnam, the Philippines and Turkey. Facebook can't afford to turn its back on these countries and their governments, so this promise, too, sounds a bit hollow.

Zuckerberg's latest promise is, indeed, one taken from a strategy textbook: Preemptively announce the intent to remake itself without abandoning the core business that funds everything. But it will mean nothing unless Zuckerberg can find a way to genuinely respect the welfare of his 2.7 billion users and improve the quality of social discourse, whether it takes place in town squares or in living rooms.

Viewpoint 4

> *"The United States, with less than 5 percent of the world's population, has 46 percent of the world's civilian-owned guns ..."*

The United States has the Highest Gun Ownership and Homicide Rate of the World's Most Developed Nations

Jonathan Masters

In the following viewpoint, Jonathan Masters delves into the issue of how gun ownership correlates to the homicide rate and compares the United States to other developed world nations. Masters demonstrates through statistics that the United States has the highest gun ownership rate in the world by population and the highest homicide rate among other developed world nations. Masters provides short summaries of gun ownership and violence in six other developed nations. Jonathan Masters has written many in-depth articles for the Council on Foreign Relations.

As you read, consider the following questions:

1. Why is the topic of gun ownership so hotly debated?
2. According to the viewpoint, in which two countries do police officers not carry weapons?

"U.S. Gun Policy: Global Comparisons" by Jonathan Masters,Council on Foreign Relations, June 10, 2022. Reprinted with permission. For more analysis and social issues and foreign policy, visit CFR.org.

3. Which country, as stated in the viewpoint, has the lowest crime rate?

The debate over gun control in the United States has waxed and waned over the years, stirred by frequent mass shootings in civilian settings. Gun violence is the leading cause of death for children and young adults in the United States. In particular, the ready availability of assault weapons and ammunition has provoked national discussion after multiple mass shootings of school children, most recently in Uvalde, Texas. However, Congress has repeatedly been unable to pass meaningful gun legislation in the wake of these tragedies despite broad public support for new restrictions.

Recent years have seen some of the worst gun violence in U.S. history. In 2021, guns killed more than forty-five thousand Americans, the highest toll in decades; and the upward trend is on track to continue.

Many gun control advocates say the United States should look to the experiences of wealthy democratic peers that have instituted tighter restrictions to curb gun violence.

United States

Gun ownership in the United States is rooted in the Second Amendment of the Constitution: "A well-regulated Militia, being necessary to the security of a free State, the right of the people to keep and bear Arms, shall not be infringed."

The United States, with less than 5 percent of the world's population, has 46 percent of the world's civilian-owned guns, according to the most recent report by the Switzerland-based Small Arms Survey (2018). It ranks number one in firearms per capita. The United States also has the highest homicide-by-firearm rate of the world's most-developed nations. Many gun rights proponents say these statistics do not indicate a causal relationship.

However, the right to bear arms is not unlimited. The U.S. Congress and state legislatures have authority to enact controlling legislation, and the U.S. Supreme Court has upheld some firearms restrictions, such as bans on concealed weapons and on the possession of certain types of weapons, as well as prohibitions on the sale of guns to certain categories of people. The Gun Control Act of 1968 prohibits individuals under eighteen years of age, convicted criminals, the mentally disabled, dishonorably discharged military personnel, and others from purchasing firearms. In 1993, the Brady Handgun Violence Prevention Act mandated background checks for all unlicensed individuals purchasing a firearm from a federally authorized dealer.

But some gun laws have not survived judicial review. For instance, in 2008, the Supreme Court struck down a Washington, DC, law that banned handguns, the court's first ruling on the Second Amendment in nearly seventy years.

Federal law provides the basis for firearms regulation in the United States, but states and cities can impose further restrictions. Some studies have indicated that states with more restrictive gun laws, such as California or Hawaii, have lower incidences of gun deaths, although researchers say more analysis is needed.

In recent years, Congress has debated changes to existing gun laws, typically in the immediate aftermath of a high-profile mass shooting, such as that in Las Vegas in 2017 (sixty people killed), or in Parkland, Florida, in 2018 (seventeen killed). But in almost every instance, legislation has failed to garner enough support. Ill-fated bills have proposed measures including an assault weapons ban, expanded background checks, and a prohibition on firearm sales to people on federal terrorism watch lists.

As of mid-2022, there were no federal laws banning semiautomatic assault weapons, military-style .50 caliber rifles, handguns, or large-capacity magazines. There was also no federal requirement for those purchasing a gun to have any firearm safety training. There was a federal prohibition on assault weapons and on large-capacity magazines between 1994 and 2004, but Congress allowed these restrictions to expire.

Meanwhile, gun violence has surged amid the COVID-19 pandemic. As of June 2022, guns have killed some nineteen thousand people in the United States this year. The majority of those were in acts of suicide. Mass shootings—those with at least four victims—were occurring at a rate of at least one per day.

Canada

Gun ownership is also relatively high in Canada, at about thirty-five firearms per hundred residents (ranking fifth globally), but the country does not struggle with a similar level of gun violence. As in the United States, Canada's national government sets gun restrictions that the provinces, territories, and municipalities can supplement. And like its southern neighbor, Canada's gun laws have often been prompted by gun violence. In 1989, a student armed with a semiautomatic rifle killed fourteen students and injured more than a dozen others at a Montreal engineering school. The incident is widely credited with driving major gun reforms that imposed a twenty-eight-day waiting period for purchases; mandatory safety training courses; more detailed background checks; bans on large-capacity magazines; and bans or greater restrictions on military-style firearms and ammunition.

Firearms in Canada are divided into three classes: nonrestricted weapons, such as ordinary rifles and shotguns; restricted, such as handguns and semiautomatic rifles or shotguns; and prohibited, such as automatic weapons. It is illegal to own a fully automatic weapon unless it was registered before 1978.

Changes to the law in 1995 required individuals to obtain a license to buy guns and ammunition, as well as register all firearms. However, in 2012, the requirement to register nonrestricted guns was dropped, and related public records were expunged. Following another mass shooting, at a Quebec City mosque in 2017, the government passed a bill to again require nonrestricted firearms to be registered and allow background checks to consider events from more than five years in the past. In 2020, after a gunman killed twenty-two people in Canada's deadliest mass shooting, Prime Minister Justin Trudeau announced a ban on "assault-style" firearms.. The legislation also required those who owned now-prohibited firearms to either participate in a buyback program or comply with a strict storage regime.

Australia

The inflection point for modern gun control in Australia was the Port Arthur massacre of 1996, when a young man killed thirty-five people and wounded nearly two dozen others. The rampage, perpetrated with a semiautomatic rifle, was the worst mass shooting in the nation's history. Less than two weeks later, the conservative-led national government pushed through fundamental changes to the country's gun laws in cooperation with the various states and territories, which regulate firearms.

The National Agreement on Firearms all but prohibited automatic and semiautomatic assault rifles, mandated licensing and registration, and instituted a temporary gun buyback program that took some 650,000 assault weapons (about one-sixth of the national stock) out of public circulation. Among other things, the law also required licensees to demonstrate a "genuine need" for a particular type of gun and take a firearm safety course. After another high-profile shooting, in Melbourne in 2002, Australia's handgun laws were tightened as well. Many analysts said these measures were highly effective, citing declines in gun-death rates and gun-related mass killings.

Following an uptick in gun sales in 2017, however, Australian gun control advocates warned against the easing of gun laws in some states and territories. The gun safety discussion was also influenced by the suspected murder-suicide of a family of seven in Western Australia, the country's worst mass shooting in two decades. Today, Australia has more guns in circulation than before the Port Arthur massacre, although the number of people who own them has fallen over the same period.

Israel

Military service is compulsory in Israel, and guns are a part of many Israelis' daily lives. Much of the population has indirect access to an assault weapon by either being a soldier or a reservist or a relative of one. By law, most eighteen-year-olds are drafted into the military, psychologically screened, and provided at least some weapons training after high school. After serving typically two or three years in the armed forces, however, most Israelis are discharged and subject to civilian gun laws.

The country has relatively strict gun regulations, including an assault-weapons ban, a requirement to register ownership with the government, and a limit of one gun per owner. To obtain a gun license, an applicant must be an Israeli citizen or permanent resident; speak at least some Hebrew, Israel's official language; and pass a health screening. The minimum-age requirements vary: twenty-seven years old for citizens with no military or national-service experience, twenty-one for those who have served, and forty-five for permanent residents who are not citizens. Applicants must also show genuine cause to carry a firearm, such as self-defense or hunting.

United Kingdom

Modern gun control efforts in the United Kingdom (UK) have also been precipitated by extraordinary acts of violence that sparked public outrage. In 1987, a lone gunman armed with two semiautomatic rifles and a handgun went on a six-hour shooting spree roughly seventy miles west of London, killing more than a dozen people and then himself. In the wake of the incident, known as the Hungerford massacre, Britain introduced the Firearms (Amendment) Act, which expanded the list of banned weapons, including certain semiautomatic rifles, and increased registration requirements for other weapons.

A gun-related tragedy in the Scottish town of Dunblane in 1996 prompted Britain's strictest gun laws yet. A man armed with four handguns shot and killed sixteen schoolchildren and one adult before committing suicide in the country's worst mass shooting to date. The incident sparked a public campaign known as the Snowdrop Petition, which helped drive legislation banning handguns, with few exceptions. The government also instituted a temporary gun buyback program, which many credit with taking tens of thousands of illegal or unwanted guns out of supply.

A large majority of police officers in the UK do not carry firearms, setting them apart from counterparts in the United States and other countries. Guns are limited to specially trained police units that respond to particular emergencies or deploy for certain types of operations. Supporters of the policy say the unarmed officer symbolizes policing of the public by consent as opposed to by force.

Norway

Gun control had rarely been much of a political issue in Norway—where gun laws are viewed as tough, but ownership rates are high—until a right-wing extremist killed seventy-seven people in attacks in Oslo and at an island summer camp in 2011. Though Norway ranks fourteenth worldwide in gun ownership, according to Small Arms Survey, it placed near the bottom in gun homicide rates. (The U.S. rate is roughly forty-four times higher.) Most Norwegian police, like the British, do not carry firearms.

In the wake of the tragedy, some analysts in the United States cited the rampage as proof that strict gun laws—which in Norway include requiring applicants to be at least eighteen years of age, specify a "valid reason" for gun ownership, and obtain a government license—are ineffective. Other gun control critics have argued that had other Norwegians, including the police, been armed, the gunman might have been stopped earlier and killed fewer victims.

After the massacre, an independent commission recommended tightening Norway's gun restrictions in various ways, including by prohibiting pistols and semiautomatic weapons, but changes were not made. In 2018, the Norwegian parliament approved a ban on semiautomatic firearms, which took effect in 2021.

Japan

Gun control advocates regularly cite Japan's highly restrictive firearm regulations in tandem with its extraordinarily low gun death rate. Most years, fewer than one hundred Japanese die from gun violence in a country of 125 million people. Most guns are illegal in the country and ownership rates, which are quite low, reflect this.

Under Japan's firearm and sword law, the only guns permitted are shotguns, air guns, guns with specific research or industrial purposes, or those used for competitions. However, before access to these specialty weapons is granted, one must obtain formal instruction and pass a battery of written, mental, and drug tests and a rigorous background check. Furthermore, owners must inform the authorities of how their weapons and ammunition are stored and provide their firearms for annual inspection.

Some analysts link Japan's aversion to firearms with its demilitarization in the aftermath of World War II. Others say that because the overall crime rate in the country is so low, most Japanese see no need for firearms.

Viewpoint 5

> *"Silent Sam and the other 700-plus Confederate statues still standing in the U.S. represent a legacy of slavery and the structural racism that followed."*

Tearing Down Confederate Statues Leaves Structural Racism Intact

Anne C. Bailey

In the following viewpoint, Anne C. Bailey argues that the tearing down of Confederate statues may do little to stem white supremacy and racist hate. Bailey notes that Confederate statues and imagery serve to reinforce white supremacy, but she questions activists' resolve to go further in their goal of eliminating racism from the fabric of American society. Anne C. Bailey is a historian at SUNY Binghamton in Binghamton, New York. Bailey's expertise includes African American, African, and Caribbean history.

As you read, consider the following questions:

1. Why was the Civil War fought, according to this historian?
2. What is this author's opinion on the removal of Confederate statues?

3. According to the author, what has to happen to end persistent hate?

When protesters tore down the "Silent Sam" Confederate statue at the University of North Carolina Chapel Hill on Aug. 20, it wasn't just destruction of state property—a crime for which the protesters are now being investigated.

Rather, the protesters knocked a powerful symbol of white supremacy from its pedestal—both literally and figuratively. Silent Sam, after all, was meant to pay tribute to those who wanted to maintain slavery.

With the backing of the state, Silent Sam has stood proudly and defiantly at UNC Chapel Hill since 1913. Now the statue has become one of many in dozens of cities and municipalities where monuments of Confederate soldiers and generals have been removed—mostly with official sanction.

But what, if anything, will this latest removal of a Confederate statue accomplish?

While the removal of Silent Sam was a joyous moment for protesters who had long requested that the university acknowledge that the statue was a divisive symbol of white supremacy—for the opposing side, it was an example of what they call the intolerance of the left, particularly among those who oppose the views and policies of President Trump.

Slavery at root of divide

This divide has deep historical roots. Silent Sam and the other 700-plus Confederate statues still standing in the U.S. represent a legacy of slavery and the structural racism that followed.

My book, "The Weeping Time: Memory and the Largest Slave Auction in American History," documented one important aspect of antebellum slavery. The harsh and devastating reality of slave auctions meant that profit mattered more than people. My book is one of many new books that seek to remind a forgetful public of America's original sin.

Beginning first in Virginia in 1662, with the other colonies and states following suit, officials enacted laws to specify that slave status followed the condition of the mother. This continued right up to the eve of the Civil War in 1861 where the enslaved were still bought and sold on the open market. And so, until the signing of the Emancipation Proclamation by Abraham Lincoln in 1863, to be black in America was synonymous with a separate and unequal status.

The American Civil War was fought to settle the question as to whether blacks should continue to be separate and unequal or whether the United States of America would finally be united—united in its commitment to the notion of justice and equality put forth in the Declaration of the Independence.

The simple fact is that the North won the war, and in winning it, the North preserved the union. The Confederate statues, therefore, represent a step backwards—a symbol of what the United States once was—not what it is now.

Averting a civil war over statues

Today, the nation is experiencing what some call a civil war over statues. The only way to avert this new civil war—in some ways a symbolic one over the outcome of the original Civil War—is to have dialogue. And after dialogue, actions must follow. It could be that protesters who toppled Silent Sam acted out of a sense that dialogue had reached a standstill after years of debate.

Communities may decide to take the statues down or replace them with monuments that honor abolitionists like Harriet Tubman, Frederick Douglass, William H. Seward or Thaddeus Stephens. They may also choose to keep the Confederate statues intact with a plaque that gives a more balanced view of the causes of the war. In this way, they would be used as a tool to teach about the Civil War—one of the bloodiest chapters in American history and one that none of us should want to repeat.

Tearing down Confederate statues may actually do little to further the goal of ending the legacy of slavery. It will not bring about systemic change or end notions of white supremacy or eradicate structural racism.

The more difficult work when it comes to dismantling the legacy of slavery involves ending some of slavery's byproducts, such as mass incarceration of black and brown bodies and systemic educational inequities for children of color. The hope is that those protesters will channel their zeal and apply it to these thorny and persistent problems. There is no easy fix. But if and when that fix does come, 100 years from now, America will be remembered not only for its technological advances—such as its computers, its robots or its driverless cars—but for its commitment to human rights.

Periodical and Internet Sources Bibliography

The following articles have been selected to supplement the diverse views presented in this chapter.

Davey Alba, "Facebook Must Better Police Online Hate, State Attorneys General Say," *The New York Times*, August 5, 2020. www.nytimes.com/2020/08/05/technology/facebook-online-hate.html.

Isheba Cornwall, "Combatting Hate Speech Through Media: A Young Caribbean Woman's Perspective," United Nations, June 14, 2022. www.un.org/en/academic-impact/countering-hate-speech-through-media-young-caribbean-woman%E2%80%99s-perspective.

Denitsa Dineva, "Six Things Social Media Users and Businesses Can Do To Combat Online Hate," *The Conversation*, March 7, 2022. theconversation.com/six-things-social-media-users-and-businesses-can-do-to-combat-hate-online-177943.

Dick Durban, "Technology Created This Monster, Only Technology Can Take It Down," The Hill, October 16, 2023. thehill.com/opinion/congress-blog/4259240-technology-created-this-monster-only-technology-can-take-it-down/.

David Hudson, "Is Hate Speech Protected by the First Amendment?" FIRE, February 8, 2022. www.thefire.org/news/hate-speech-protected-first-amendment?.

Quinta Jurecic, "The Kids Online Safety Act and the State of Tech Policy," Lawfare, March 27, 2024. www.lawfaremedia.org/article/the-kids-online-safety-act-and-the-state-of-tech-policy.

Maya Kornberg, "Congress is Woefully Unprepared to Regulate Tech," Brennan Center for Justice, July 5, 2023. www.brennancenter.org/our-work/analysis-opinion/congress-woefully-unprepared-regulate-tech.

Sylvia Lu, "Tech Law in 2025: A Look Ahead at AI, Privacy and Social Media Regulation Under the New Trump Administration," *The Conversation*, January 3, 2025. theconversation.com/tech-law-in-2025-a-look-ahead-at-ai-privacy-and-social-media-regulation-under-the-new-trump-administration-245425.

Barbara Ortutay, "Meta Roles Back Hate Speech Rules as Zuckerberg Sites 'Recent Elections' as a Catalyst," AP, January 8,2025. apnews.

com/article/meta-facebook-hate-speech-trump-immigrant-transgender-41191638cd7c720b950c05f9395a2b49.

Catherine O'Regan, "Hate Speech Regulation on Social Media: An Intractable Contemporary Challenge," Research Outreach, February 26, 2020. researchoutreach.org/articles/hate-speech-regulation-social-media-intractable-contemporary-challenge/.

John Samples, "Counter-Speech Offers an Effective Remedy for 'Hate Speech'" CATO Institute, June 1, 2018. www.cato.org/blog/counter-speech-offers-effective-remedy-hate-speech.

Aarti Shahani, "From Hate Speech to Fake News: The Content Crisis Facing Mark Zuckerberg," NPR, November 17, 2016. www.npr.org/sections/alltechconsidered/2016/11/17/495827410/from-hate-speech-to-fake-news-the-content-crisis-facing-mark-zuckerberg.

Lindsey Shelton, "How Meta's Policy Updates Could Encourage Hate and Threaten Democracy," Southern Poverty Law Center, January 24, 2025. www.splcenter.org/resources/stories/meta-policy-updates-could-encourage-hate-threaten-democracy/.

Nadine Strossen, "Hate: Why We Should Resist It with Free Speech, Not Censorship," CATO Institute, May 21, 2018. www.cato.org/multimedia/cato-daily-podcast/hate-why-we-should-resist-it-free-speech-not-censorship.

For Further Discussion

Chapter 1

1. Several viewpoints in chapter one maintain that alt-right groups in the US are increasing. What factors are playing a part in this resurgence?
2. How is the hatred of Roma, Gypsy, or Traveller communities similar to or different from hatred of the Jewish community?
3. Has hatred of the Jewish community changed throughout history? If yes, in what ways?

Chapter 2

1. Both President Donald Trump and Governor George Wallace were shot at in their careers. Compare and contrast the results of the two.
2. How does political language influence voters? What can individuals do to challenge this?
3. What is the history of the Israeli-Palestinian conflict? Does this conflict currently affect hate speech?

Chapter 3

1. Using viewpoint two, compare and contrast your education with the typical education of boys and girls from Nazi Germany.
2. Might media and/or media influencers affect cultural beliefs or actions by teens and pre-teens on others? Use facts from viewpoint articles to back up your claims.
3. Are there ways for individuals to resist hate speech and hate groups? Give examples of how could this be done using social media.

Chapter 4

1. Can hate be prevented? Use evidence from two different viewpoint articles to back up your argument.

2. Use the viewpoint in this chapter to compare Facebook and WhatsApp. Which platform is more private? Which is more public? How does this affect hate speech?
3. While not as high as in the US, the level of gun ownership in Canada is high compared to many other countries. Why do you suppose that the rate of gun violence is lower in Canada than in the US?

Organizations to Contact

The editors have compiled the following list of organizations concerned with the issues debated in this book. The descriptions are derived from materials provided by the organizations. All have publications or information available for interested readers. The list was compiled on the date of publication of the present volume; the information provided here may change. Be aware that many organizations take several weeks or longer to respond to inquiries, so allow as much time as possible.

Anti-Defamation League

605 Third Avenue
New York, NY 10158
phone: 212-885-7700
email: use form on contact page
website: www.adl.org

The ADL is one of the leading nonpartisan anti-hate organizations in the world. The ADL fights against all kinds of hatred, antisemitism, bigotry, and extremism. Visitors to its website can follow research, read articles, and sign up for email updates. They can also find out how to take action against hate, antisemitism, and extremism.

CATO Institute

1000 Massachusetts Avenue NW
Washington, DC 2000
phone: 202-842-0200
email: use form on contact page
website: www.cato.org

The CATO Institute is an independent organization dedicated to principles and values instead of politics and partisanship. On the organization's website, visitors can read blog posts and articles, listen to podcasts, watch video clips discussing topical issues, and sign up for a newsletter.

Center for American Progress (CAP)

1333 H Street NW, Suite 100E
Washington, DC 20005
phone: 202-682-1611
email: use form on contact page
website: www.americanprogress.org

The Center for American Progress is an independent, nonpartisan, policy institute dedicated to improving the lives of all Americans. Besides reading about issues, learning how to take action, and joining the email newsletter, interested persons can join live webinar events hosted by CAP featuring experts on import issues which will inform.

Council on Foreign Relations

58 East 68th Street, New York, NY 10065
Phone 212-434-9400
email: communications@cfr.org
website: www.cfr.org

The Council on Foreign Relations is an independent nonpartisan organization and think tank which promotes discussion of pressing issues facing the United States and the world. It hosts the Center for Preventative Action, which has information about the issues of hate speech and hate groups.

The Foundation for Individual Rights and Expression (FIRE)

P.O. Box 40128
Philadelphia, PA 19106
phone: 215-717-FIRE
email: fire@thefire.org
website: www.thefire.org

The FIRE was founded over two decades ago and has become a leader in defending fundamental rights on college campuses. The organization's chief mission is to defend and promote free speech for all Americans. Its website provides articles, videos, the latest news, and a newsletter to inform others on how to protect freedom of speech for all.

The Leadership Conference

1620 L Street NW, Suite 1100
Washington, DC 20036
phone: 202-466-3311
email: use form on contact page
website: civilrights.org

Since 1950, The Leadership Conference has tirelessly worked for civil rights and social justice. This site includes resources to support the rights of individuals by taking action against hate and bias.

Southern Poverty Law Center

400 Washington Avenue
Montgomery, AL 36104
phone: 334-956-8200
email: use form on contact page
website: www.splcenter.org

The Southern Poverty Law Center is an organization that works to promote equality across the US, seeks to diminish discrimination and oppression, and monitors hate groups and hate speech. Interested readers can learn about the latest issues and read a comprehensive yearly report monitoring hate and extremist groups in the United States.

UNESCO

885 Second Avenue, 30th Floor
New York, NY 10017
phone: 917-810-9030
email: newyork@unesco.org
website: www.unesco.org/en

UNESCO is a global organization with offices in New York. Along with its member states across the globe, UNESCO is a specialized agency dedicated to fostering equality and peace through communication, education, science, and culture. Find a trove of resources on this site, including up-to-date information on hate speech and hate groups.

UNICEF USA

125 Maiden Lane
New York, NY 10038
phone: 800-367-5437
website: www.unicefusa.org

The United Nations International Children's Emergency Fund (UNICEF) was created to help children and mothers affected by World War II. Today its mission is to pursue an equitable world for every child. Individuals can learn how to help the world's children by reading feature stories, fundraising, and fighting against hate and injustice.

US Department of Justice

950 Pennsylvania Avenue NW
Washington, DC 20530
phone: 202-514-2000
email: use form on contact page
website: www.justice.gov

The US Department of Justice has a mission to uphold the rule of law, protect civil rights, and keep America safe. This website has information about hate speech and hate groups in the US, although it may not be up to date. Individuals may also take action using links on the main page to report crimes, report missing persons, find help for victims, and more.

Bibliography of Books

Carol Anderson. *We Are Not Yet Equal: Understanding Our Racial Divide.* New York, NY: Bloomsbury, 2018.

Susan Campbell Bartoletti. *They Called Themselves the KKK: The Birth of an American Terrorist Group.* Boston, MA: Houghton Mifflin, 2010.

Crystal Marie Fleming. *Rise UP!: How You Can Join the Fight Against White Supremacy.* New York, NY: Henry Holt & Company, 2021.

Philip S. Gorski. *The Flag and the Cross: White Christian Nationalism and the Threat to American Democracy.* New York, NY: Oxford University Press, 2022.

Marcia S. Gresko. *How Should Extremist Content Be Regulated on Social Media?* San Diego, CA: Reference Point Press, 2021.

Jean Guerrero. *Hatemonger: Stephen Miller, Donald Trump, and the White Nationalist Agenda.* New York, NY: William Morrow, an Imprint of Harper Collins Publishers, 2020.

Kristina Lyn Heitkamp. *Confronting Anti-Semitism.* New York, NY: Rosen YA, 2018.

Yassmin Abdel-Magied. *Stand Up and Speak Out Against Racism.* Somerville, MA: Walker Books, 2024.

Michael Miller. *Exposing Hate: Prejudice, Hate, and Violence in Action.* Minneapolis, MN: Twenty-First Century Books, 2019.

Alex Novak. *Hate and Intolerance.* Buffalo, NY: Rosen Publishing, 2023.

Christian Picciolini. *Breaking Hate: Confronting the New Culture of Extremism*

Layla F. Saad. *Me and White Supremacy.* Naperville, IL: Sourcebooks Explore, 2022.

Deanna Singh. *A Smart Girl's Guide: Race & Inclusion: Standing Up to Racism and Building a Better World.* Middleton, WI: American Girl Publishing, 2021.

Juan M. Floyd-Thomas. *Critical Race Theology: White Supremacy, American Christianity, and the Ongoing Culture Wars.* Maryknoll, NY: Orbis Books, 2024.

Jeremy Waldron. *The Harm in Hate Speech.* Cambridge, MA: Harvard University Press, 2012.

Index

L

M

N

O

P

R

S

T

U

V

W